The Exchange Rate System and the IMF: A Modest Agenda

MORRIS GOLDSTEIN

The Exchange Rate System and the IMF: A Modest Agenda

INSTITUTE FOR INTERNATIONAL ECONOMICS
Washington, DC
June 1995

Morris Goldstein, Senior Fellow, has held several senior staff positions at the International Monetary Fund (1970–94), including Deputy Director of its Research Department (1987–94). He has written extensively on international economic policy and on international capital markets. He is coauthor of "The Integration of World Capital Markets" (Federal Reserve Bank of Kansas City, 1994), *Exchange Rate Management and International Capital Flows* (IMF, 1993), *Policy Issues in the Evolving International Monetary System* (IMF, 1992), *The Determinants and Systemic Consequences of International Capital Flows* (IMF, 1991), and *International Policy Coordination and Exchange Rate Fluctuations* (University of Chicago Press, 1990).

INSTITUTE FOR INTERNATIONAL ECONOMICS
11 Dupont Circle, NW
Washington, DC 20036-1207
(202) 328-9000 FAX: (202) 328-0900

C. Fred Bergsten, *Director*
Christine F. Lowry, *Director of Publications*

Typesetting by Automated Graphic Systems
Printing by Automated Graphic Systems

Printed in the United States of America
97 96 95   5 4 3 2 1

Library of Congress Cataloging-in-Publication Data

Goldstein, Morris, 1944–
    The exchange rate system and the IMF : a modest agenda / Morris Goldstein.
        p. cm. — (Policy analyses in international economics ; 39)
        Includes bibliographical references.
        1. Foreign exchange administration.   2. International Monetary Fund.   I. Title.   II. Series.
    HG3815.G65   1995   95-17292
    332.1'52—dc20   CIP

ISBN 0-88132-219-9

Marketed and Distributed outside the USA and Canada by Longman Group UK Limited, London

Contents

Preface

The Institute for International Economics has published extensively on reform of the international monetary system. John Williamson and I developed the concept of currency target zones in 1982 in our chapter "Exchange Rates and Trade Policy" in William R. Cline, ed., *Trade Policy in the 1980s* (1983). Williamson subsequently elaborated the target zone idea (*The Exchange Rate System*, 1983 and revised 1985) and, with Marcus Miller, extended it to provide a comprehensive "blueprint" for international economic policy coordination (*Targets and Indicators: A Blueprint for the International Coordination of Economic Policy*, 1987).

The Group of Seven major industrial democracies (G-7) adopted the target zone idea in 1987 under the label of "reference ranges." But that regime was not maintained for long and current G-7 officials are clearly reluctant to repeat the effort, let alone adopt a more ambitious scheme like the "blueprint." The international monetary system continues to experience periodic difficulties, however, and its improvement could bolster the prospects for global prosperity and stability. Hence the Institute concluded that it should develop and propose a more modest set of proposals that could both improve global economic performance and stand a chance of early adoption. The present volume offers those suggestions.

The new study was prepared by Morris Goldstein, who recently became a Senior Fellow at the Institute. Dr. Goldstein spent the previous 24 years with the Research Department of the International Monetary Fund, the last eight as its Deputy Director. Hence he is uniquely qualified to assess the need, and potential, for changes in the operation of the Fund and the international monetary system more broadly. We hope that his analysis and recommendations will be helpful to the G-7 summit that will be considering reform of the international economic institutions at its forthcoming meeting in Halifax, Canada, in June 1995.

The Institute for International Economics is a private nonprofit institution for the study and discussion of international economic policy. Its purpose is to analyze important issues in that area and to develop and communicate practical new approaches for dealing with them. The Institute is completely nonpartisan.

The Institute is funded largely by philanthropic foundations. Major institutional grants are now being received from the German Marshall Fund of the United States, which created the Institute with a generous commitment of funds in 1981, and from the Ford Foundation, the William and Flora Hewlett Foundation, the William M. Keck, Jr. Foundation, the Korea Foundation, the Andrew Mellon Foundation, the C. V. Starr Foundation, and the United States–Japan Foundation. A number of other foundations and private corporations also contribute to the highly diversified financial resources of the Institute. About 12 percent of the Institute's resources in our latest fiscal year were provided by contributors outside the United States, including about 5 percent from Japan.

The Board of Directors bears overall responsibility for the Institute and gives general guidance and approval to its research program—including identification of topics that are likely to become important to international economic policymakers over the medium run (generally, one to three years), and which thus should be addressed by the Institute. The Director, working closely with the staff and outside Advisory Committee, is responsible for the development of particular projects and makes the final decision to publish an individual study.

The Institute hopes that its studies and other activities will contribute to building a stronger foundation for international economic policy around the world. We invite readers of these publications to let us know how they think we can best accomplish this objective.

C. FRED BERGSTEN
Director
May 1995

Acknowledgments

I am most grateful to the following colleagues for their helpful suggestions on all or part of an earlier draft of this study: Tam Bayoumi, Ralph Bryant, Peter Clark, David Coe, Max Corden, Charles Dallara, David Folkerts-Landau, Wendy Dobson, Hali Edison, Barry Eichengreen, Robert Feldman, Stanley Fischer, Jeffrey Frankel, Monty Graham, Graham Hacche, Gary Hufbauer, Peter Isard, Peter Kenen, Alexandre Kafka, Catherine Mann, Michael Mussa, Jacques Polak, Marcus Noland, J. David Richardson, Ted Truman, and John Williamson. I owe a special debt of gratitude to C. Fred Bergsten, who in addition to offering valuable comments on the entire manuscript provided continuing encouragement for the undertaking itself. Thanks also go to Albert Kim for his research assistance, and to the publications staff of the Institute for helping to produce the study (under a very tight deadline). I of course remain solely responsible for any errors and omissions that remain in the book.

1

Overview and Conclusions

Rationale for the Study

1995 already shows indications of being an eventful year for global currency markets. In April, the US dollar reached record lows against both the yen and the deutsche mark.[1] In Europe, while there have been no crises on the scale of those that rocked the Exchange Rate Mechanism (ERM) of the European Monetary System (EMS) in the fall of 1992 and the summer of 1993, renewed tensions led in early March to the devaluations of both the Spanish peseta and the Portuguese escudo. Jacques Santer, the new president of the European Commission, has expressed his concerns about instabilities and misalignments in global currency markets and has called for a return to the spirit of the Plaza and Louvre agreements to revive international economic policy coordination.[2]

---

1. Note that the change in the dollar's overall, trade-weighted exchange rate (the so-called effective exchange rate) has been much less marked than suggested by the depreciations against the yen and the deutsche mark. Specifically, as of 21 April 1995 the dollar was down (relative to its end-1994 value) by 16 and 11 percent against the yen and the deutsche mark, respectively, versus 8 percent against industrial-country currencies overall (according to the IMF's index of nominal effective exchange rates). Looking at exchange rate developments in terms of real effective exchange rates—that is, nominal exchange rates adjusted for inflation differences among countries—tells a broadly similar story. If the index of effective exchange rates was more comprehensive and included developing-country currencies as well, the contrast between the effective exchange rate for the dollar and bilateral rates against the yen and the deutsche mark would be even more striking.

2. See Santer (1995). By "misalignment," I mean a departure of the real exchange rate from the level consistent with economic fundamentals.

1

The commotion has not been confined to the currencies of the major industrial countries. The turn of the year witnessed the unfolding of the Mexican economic crisis. After being forced by market pressures to devalue and shortly thereafter to float, the Mexican peso suffered a sharp decline and at this writing is trading at slightly less than 60 percent of its precrisis value against the US dollar. As in the wake of earlier crises in the ERM, the Mexican crisis has also raised questions about the adequacy of existing "early warning" arrangements.

In mid-June 1995, the Group of Seven (G-7) heads of state and government will get together in Halifax for their annual economic summit. Among other things, they are scheduled to discuss a report on the role of the international financial institutions.[3] It would not be surprising or amiss if their discussions included a review of the functioning of the exchange rate system and of the surveillance functions of the International Monetary Fund (IMF). Yet even after a concentrated period of reflection, prompted in part by the 50th anniversary of the Bretton Woods conference, there is little agreement on what to do about the exchange rate system. All appraisals conclude that the performance of the world economy could be improved if policy discipline were strengthened and if the frequency and size of exchange rate misalignments could be reduced. But there is little consensus on how to bring that about. Those most convinced of the need for fundamental reform of the system—in the sense of a move to explicit, binding exchange rate targets by the three key-currency countries—are not in a position to do much about it. Those who are in such a position are not convinced of the need for such fundamental reform. Much the same could be said for proposals to give the IMF greater responsibilities in overseeing exchange rate policies and in organizing international economic policy coordination. More limited changes in the operation and/or institutional architecture of the system would presumably stand a greater chance of being implemented. But what specific changes should those be? And if implemented, would these limited changes make enough of a difference to the system's performance to be worth undertaking?

Key Recommendations

This monograph sets out a modest agenda for both managing the exchange rate system and strengthening the IMF's (de facto) oversight responsibilities. I use the adjective "modest" for two reasons. First, the set of proposals advanced here does not require the key-currency countries to announce

---

3. The summit communiqué issued at the conclusion of the Naples economic summit in July 1994 notes that participants are conscious of their responsibility to "renew and revitalize" the Bretton Woods institutions and have agreed to focus in Halifax next year on, inter alia, "what framework of institutions will be required to meet [these] challenges in the 21st century. . . ."

binding exchange rate targets or to adopt rules or guidelines for macroeconomic policy coordination more generally; nor does it envisage amendment to the IMF's Articles of Agreement, or significant changes in the IMF's governance, or even a substantial diminution of the G-7's role in international economic policy coordination. In fact, it argues that these "fundamental" reforms are not really needed—and could well be counterproductive—for achieving improvements in the functioning of the system. Second, the agenda is modest in the improvement that it can realistically be expected to make to the functioning of the exchange rate system. This is an evolutionary—not revolutionary—approach to reform. That said, I would regard a modest improvement as worth pursuing—particularly since the main alternatives appear either impractical, or undesirable, or both.

The key recommendations underlying this modest agenda can be summarized as follows:

- **Management of the exchange rate system ought to focus on avoiding large misalignments** (particularly for the key currencies) **rather than on trying to reduce short-run variability of nominal and real exchange rates.**

- **Under present arrangements, needed exchange rate and accompanying policy adjustments are delayed too long, with the result that large misalignments occur more frequently and last longer than they should.** This happens under both fixed and flexible exchange rate regimes (albeit for different reasons).

- **Dealing with this problem will require both a consistent and credible exchange rate policy on the part of the three key-currency countries and enhanced "early warning" arrangements for the system as a whole. The IMF is well placed to assist in these efforts**: it has more political independence than governments have, as well as the necessary technical resources and focus for evaluating exchange rate developments and related macroeconomic policy requirements. The Fund also can contribute to improved market discipline by facilitating the information flow to markets and by sharing more of its own assessment of policy fundamentals with these markets.

- **On exchange rate policy, the G-3 countries (along with their G-7 colleagues) should pledge to monitor exchange rate developments closely and be willing both to engage in concerted intervention and to shift the course of monetary policy away from domestic priorities in those unusual circumstances when there is, by common consent, a large misalignment of their currencies.**[4] They should keep their estimates of equilibrium exchange rates quiet.

---

4. Exchange rate policy also needs to be supported over the longer term by an appropriate fiscal policy, although for reasons laid out in chapter 3, it is impractical to regard fiscal policy as a tool of exchange rate management.

In contrast to more ambitious exchange rate commitments, such an exchange rate policy is credible because it is consistent with the demonstrated priority accorded to the internal objectives of monetary policy in the lion's share of circumstances. Only when misalignments are large will this priority be overturned. This policy also recognizes the substantial uncertainties surrounding the estimation of equilibrium exchange rates, the desirability of relying on the market for exchange rate judgments most of the time, and the need for the authorities to pick their spots and to act together when challenging the views of private-market participants. Relative to past performance, the aim is to be more vigilant and systematic in identifying the more serious cases of government and/or market failure and to be more consistent in implementing concerted corrective action.

■ **A series of complementary steps by industrial countries and the IMF is required to build a better early warning system:**
The IMF must (1) prepare itself better to offer a view on misalignments and associated policy adjustments in real time, (2) put forth that view (at first, confidentially) even when authorities have not asked for it, (3) increase the frequency and depth of its contacts with private capital markets (so it is more aware of market concerns), and (4) get the Interim Committee more involved in monitoring the follow-up to IMF country policy recommendations.

The major industrial countries need to (1) give the Fund the opportunity to have its view on exchange rates heard in forums where, and at the times when, exchange rate and intervention policies are being evaluated by senior policymakers; (2) make discussion of exchange rate misalignments, *cum* IMF technical support and assessment, a regular feature of each G-7 meeting (at both the ministerial and deputy ministerial level), as well as of each meeting of the relevant European Union committees dealing with exchange rate and intervention matters; and (3) hold the IMF "accountable" for its track record on identifying large misalignments and associated policy inadequacies.

Private capital markets cannot be expected to price risk appropriately unless they have the right information. While that information is for the most part widely available for industrial countries, there is scope for considerable improvement on the part of many developing countries. In addition, the ability of markets to gauge the conduct of monetary, fiscal, and structural policies in individual countries (industrial and developing alike) would likely be improved by having increased and more timely access to independent evaluation of policies and prospects by the official sector. The IMF can help on both counts. **The Fund can alter the incentives that countries have to improve the transparency, regularity, and timeliness of published economic data.**

The Fund should also move to timely publication of its Article IV staff appraisals for individual countries.[5]

■ The increased clout and agility of private capital markets is here to stay. If Fund surveillance is going to be effective in influencing the policies of large-market borrowers—be they industrial or developing countries—it will increasingly need to operate via its effect on the private market's assessment of a country's economic policies. The Fund should be both listening and speaking more to private capital markets than it has in the past.

Persuasion based on the Fund's confidential advice and the leverage associated with the Fund's own financial resources will still count, but not as much as in the past when private capital flows made up less of host countries' financing needs and exerted less potential disciplinary pressure on errant country policies.

■ Given the increasing weight of non–G-7 countries (especially developing countries) in world output, trade, and international capital markets, it is desirable to find a way in which the views of non–G-7 countries can be brought to bear on the economic policy decisions of the G-7—but without forcing the G-7 to give up the smallness and informality that they regard as so helpful to their coordination efforts. A simple way to do this is to have the host of each G-7 meeting meet with the Fund's Executive Board a few days before, as well as few days after the meeting, to hear their concerns and suggestions and to give them a summary of the meeting's main conclusions.[6]

■ Finally, the IMF and its members should reexamine the concepts of "exchange rate manipulation" and "unfair competitive advantage" to determine if and how they can be made operationally useful in a world in which almost all countries intervene in exchange markets and follow different paces and practices on capital-market liberalization.

Just as countries have by now become accustomed to bringing their trade complaints to the General Agreement on Tariffs and Trade (GATT)—and soon to the World Trade Organization (WTO)—they should be encouraged to bring their concerns and complaints on exchange rate policy to the Fund, so that these concerns can be discussed

---

5. Since November 1994, the Fund has been making publicly available that part of its Article IV country reports that describe recent economic developments, conditional upon the country giving its consent to publication. Thus far, reports for over 40 member countries have been made publicly available. The proposal outlined above would make available for publication the other part of those reports that gives the Fund's *assessment* of the country's economic policies and prospects.

6. A variant of this proposal (that would retain its simplicity) would be for the Fund's managing director to perform this function.

and evaluated on a multilateral basis. This is preferable to bilateral interpretations of manipulation and unfair competitive advantage.

Plan of the Study

The rest of the manuscript is organized along the following lines. Chapter 2 provides a survey of recent proposals for reforming the international monetary system and/or altering the responsibilities of the IMF, and it outlines the initial reaction of policy authorities to these proposals. Chapter 3 then lays out the rationale for, and the key elements of, the modest agenda for the exchange rate system and the IMF. An annex considers the theoretical and empirical literature on the link between short-run variability of exchange rates, on the one hand, and trade, investment, and economic growth in industrial countries on the other.

2

Recent Reform Proposals

Anyone who was concerned that 1994, the 50th anniversary year of the Bretton Woods conference, might have quietly slipped by without due reflection on current and future international monetary arrangements needn't have worried.

In July 1994, the Bretton Woods Commission issued its eagerly awaited report, *Bretton Woods: Looking to the Future*, replete with commission report, staff review, and over 30 background papers prepared by experts in the field.[1] Much of that report, as well as fully a third of the background papers, deals with reform of international monetary arrangements and of the IMF itself. In September, the Institute for International Economics published the proceedings of its own conference, *Managing the World Economy: Fifty Years After Bretton Woods* (Kenen 1994a). Again, the design of the international monetary system and the appropriate role of the IMF in overseeing that system featured prominently in the debate. Last October at the annual meetings in Madrid, the Bretton Woods twins themselves got in the act, hosting a conference on "Fifty Years After Bretton Woods: The Future of the IMF and the World Bank." There, too, academics and current and former policymakers laid out their visions and assessments of optimal international monetary arrangements, of the track record of G-7 policy coordination, and of the appropriate scope of the IMF's oversight responsibilities. The last few months have brought forth even further reflections, including a report by IMF staff on constraints and possibilities for improving the international monetary system (Mussa et al. 1994a) and

---

1. Bretton Woods Commission (1994a).

a book by a prominent academic on international monetary arrangements for the 21st century (Eichengreen 1994).

Much of the recent debate has focused on two questions. First, would economic performance in the major industrial countries be improved if authorities adopted explicit, binding exchange rate targets of one kind or another? Second, should management of international macroeconomic policy coordination and of exchange rate surveillance be organized through the IMF rather than (as currently is the case) by the G-7 countries themselves?

The range of answers supplied to these questions, even in the literature of the past few years, is diverse enough to make hazardous any attempt at a shorthand summary. Nevertheless, at least three strands in the recent debate merit explicit mention.

The Target Zone School

First, there is the target zone school. Its members often begin from the premise that both of the corner solutions—namely, free (or lightly managed) floating and fixed exchange rates—have been tried and found wanting. In this connection, they point to the huge dollar overvaluation of the mid-1980s under close to free floating, to the futile attempts under fixed but adjustable rates to defend disequilibrium rates during the last year(s) of both Bretton Woods and the narrow-margin ERM, and to the dramatic drop in industrial-country growth rates with the passage from the Bretton Woods regime (1950–73) to the era of managed floating (1973–94). They also regard the ad hoc G-7 policy coordination arrangements in force since the Plaza Agreement of 1985 as a distinctly inferior substitute for a more formal, rules-based approach to policy coordination.

A key element of that approach would be agreement on a set of target zones for the major currencies. The zones would be adjusted over time to reflect both differential inflation rates and changes in real economic conditions that altered real equilibrium exchange rates (Williamson 1985; Bergsten and Williamson 1994). Negotiation, maintenance, and publication of these zones would allegedly help to discipline otherwise badly behaved governments and markets, thereby reducing exchange rate volatility and misalignments.[2]

The Bretton Woods Commission (1994a) took what might be called an Augustinian approach to target zones (recall Saint Augustine's request to the Lord to make him chaste—but "not yet"). It recommended the consideration of "flexible exchange rate bands"—but only *after* the major

---

2. Volcker and Gyohten (1992) come out in favor of announced target zones as part of their own modest agenda.

industrial-country governments strengthen their macroeconomic policies and achieve greater economic convergence, and establish a more formal system of coordination to support these policy improvements. Another Augustinian target zone advocate is Kenen (1994b), who has argued that both fiscal consolidation and improvements in the policymaking process that would impart more flexibility to fiscal policy are necessary before monetary policy can be redeployed with the aim of achieving greater exchange rate stability.[3]

Bergsten (1994b) has taken an opposite tack. He claims that there are no historical examples of successful international macroeconomic policy coordination in the absence of prior or simultaneous agreement on exchange rate targets.[4] He therefore proposes that target zones be established first, as an impetus to the evolution of an effective policy coordination regime.[5] Larosiere (1994) has suggested consideration of a rules-based target zone regime, although his emphasis is more on the need for an incentive and sanction framework to ensure that countries abide by these rules than on the specification of the rules themselves.

The Corners School

A second notable class of proposals rejects the premise that the future belongs to intermediate exchange rate regimes. Indeed, the "corners" school goes in precisely the opposite direction, maintaining that the only viable options for the future are the corner exchange rate regimes—namely, (managed) floating and monetary unification (a single currency). Countries will choose which corner to go to based on familiar optimal currency area criteria (e.g., degree of openness, factor mobility, diversification of the production structure) and on their degree of monetary policy (anti-inflationary) credibility. These considerations suggest that the three key-currency countries—the United States, Germany, and Japan—should opt for managed floating and that many smaller industrial countries and most developing countries should eventually choose to become part of a currency area.

---

3. Solomon (1994) has gone further, arguing that what is needed is fiscal policy reform—not reform of the international monetary system.

4. In contrast, he sees several examples of successful policy coordination around exchange rate targets, including Bretton Woods and the EMS.

5. Moving further along the spectrum, Williamson has in a series of papers (Williamson and Miller 1987; Williamson and Henning 1994) recommended that target zones be established as part of a larger "blueprint" for economic policy coordination. The blueprint is basically a set of assignment strategies for the conduct of monetary, fiscal, and intervention policy so as to achieve internal and external balance and to keep exchange rates within wide target zones.

Eichengreen (1994) posits that explicit, binding exchange rate targets will become less and less viable because high international capital mobility limits the ability of governments to contain market pressures at acceptable political cost, because the institutionalized structure of labor markets will limit their capacity to adjust to shocks (thereby increasing the comparative advantage of the nominal exchange rate in altering relative prices), and because the increasingly political environment in which monetary policy is made will erode the credibility of monetary rules. Thus, according to Eichengreen, contingent policy rules to hit exchange rate targets—be they fixed-but-adjustable rates à la the ERM, or loud target zones à la Bergsten and Williamson (1994)—will not be credible. Managed floating is alleged to cope better with market pressures, with the need for relative price adjustments, and with lapses of monetary policy discipline. A single currency likewise is said to be less vulnerable because it is harder to undo than other exchange rate commitments, and market participants know it.

Crockett (1994) has also staked out a corners position, at least as regards the strategy for moving from the ERM to European Economic and Monetary Union (EMU). He concludes that it is only under floating and under truly fixed rates that large capital flows are apt to be stabilizing rather than destabilizing. He therefore counsels countries in the EMS to maintain floating rates during a period in which they are establishing a track record of price stability and then to jump to hard exchange rate constraints only when the prospective need for exchange rate adjustments has been virtually eliminated. In some recent writings (Goldstein and Mussa 1994; Frenkel and Goldstein 1992), I too have espoused a corners strategy by calling for a "two-tier" evolution of the exchange rate system. Here, exchange rate commitments among the three key-currency countries would be softer and quieter (i.e., managed floating) than those elsewhere (where many countries would choose to join budding currency areas). The main argument is this: Monetary policy in the three anchor countries will likely continue to be oriented toward domestic rather than external considerations—appropriately so, given the lack of other policy instruments for dealing with inflationary pressures and the business cycle. Thus, more ambitious exchange rate commitments that presuppose otherwise are not apt to carry the credibility they need to be effective. Traditional criteria for optimal currency areas, as well as anti-inflationary track records, also provide relatively low incentives for the three largest countries to take on hard exchange rate commitments with respect to one another. The ultimate corners plan is that of Cooper (1988). His preferred exchange rate regime sits on only one corner, not two—namely, a single world currency. In brief, Cooper argues that exchange rate variability along the dimensions commonly now experienced will ultimately prove unacceptably costly to businesses and that the future pattern of shocks hitting the industrial economies is likely to be more symmetric than typically assumed.

Institutional Locus for Surveillance and Coordination

Strand number three in the recent literature deals with the preferred institutional locus for exchange rate surveillance and for international macroeconomic policy coordination more generally. A leading issue here is whether the effectiveness of these oversight and coordination functions could be increased by transferring to the IMF some activities the G-7 now carries out. A related question is what changes would be required in the operation and governance of the IMF to permit it to assume those increased responsibilities.

The Bretton Woods Commission (1994a) concludes that ad hoc G-7 policy coordination arrangements have contributed to unsatisfactory long-term economic performance, that a sustained effort is needed to improve the policy coordination process, and that this process should be centralized in the IMF. The commission maintains that a problem with continuing to rely on the G-7 is that the G-7 process is not an institution, a continuing body, or an executive entity; its mandate is also too broad to permit it to focus effectively on economic and monetary issues. The IMF is seen as better-suited to that task because of its global representation, its legitimacy, and its expertise. Moreover, it is noted that the G-7 countries are in any case the Fund's major shareholders.

Dobson (1994a, 1994b, 1991) has likewise concluded that the G-7 policy coordination process needs to be reformed. She claims that the G-7 never was clear about what kind of exchange rate regime it wanted, that it suffered from both lack of continuity among major players and absence of accountability, and that the analytical nature of the exercise was ad hoc and confused. Peer pressure did not succeed in producing major policy changes. To improve the analytical framework for the exercise, she proposes participation by central bank deputies in preministerial consultations and creation of a more formalized secretariat. The IMF would provide the secretariat. More radical reforms include taking policy coordination out of the G-7 economic summit and placing it in the hands of an overhauled IMF, or even making the G-7 a candidate for "creative destruction." As Dobson (1994a, 1994b) notes, however, prospects for such radical reforms are dim because they undermine informality and frankness, the most valued aspects of the G-7 in the eyes of ministers.

Shultz (1995) and Schulmann (1994) have opted for the other corner on institutional architecture by proposing, respectively, that the IMF's exchange rate surveillance role be eliminated (now that the system has floating exchange rates),[6] or that the IMF be kept alive only as "a fleet in drydock" (as the nucleus of a future world central bank, albeit a bank not created until the second half of the 21st century).

---

6. Shultz argues that the IMF and World Bank should be merged and that they be given a new mission that emphasizes the encouragement of private investment and foreign trade.

A related set of proposals casts the institutional issue less as an either-or choice (between the G-7 and the Fund) and more as a problem of finding a compromise in policy coordination between efficiency, informality, and proximity to decision making on the one hand, and legitimacy, universality, and technical expertise on the other. Collective action is generally regarded as less likely the larger and more heterogeneous the coordinating group. Large, powerful countries will only go so far in sharing decision making over key macroeconomic and exchange rate policies. The G-7 industrial democracies will continue to account for a major share of world economic activity and finance for the foreseeable future. Thus the G-7 format can be said to reflect these realities.

At the same time, the IMF carries the legitimacy attendant to a global institution designed explicitly to oversee the international monetary system. With its growing economic weight, the non–G-7 part of the world (particularly the developing countries' part) has a legitimate interest in G-7 policies and exchange rates that affect the international economic environment in which they too must operate, and the Fund has the continuity and staff resources to handle the analytical demands of the exercise.

How can that circle then be squared? Williamson and Henning (1994) and Bergsten (1994b) have suggested that the G-7 remain the initial locus in which exchange rate and macroeconomic policy bargains are agreed, but that the G-7 seek endorsement of the appropriate bodies of the IMF before implementing these decisions. They also propose, inter alia, that the G-7 give the IMF more responsibility than it currently has for preparing analytical material for G-7 meetings. For example, if the regime was a target zone system, the Fund would assist in the calculation of equilibrium exchange rates.

Many of those who favor increasing the role of the Fund in policy coordination and exchange rate surveillance believe that the Fund would have to alter its focus, governance, and operating modalities to undertake this task effectively. The Bretton Woods Commission's view is that the Fund should "return to its roots" by shifting its main focus back to international monetary issues and to macroeconomic adjustment issues for all its membership. Longer-term development issues should be left to the World Bank Group and other development agencies. Fischer (1994) has argued that to increase the effectiveness of Fund surveillance, the Fund should concentrate on improving its macroeconomic policy analysis so that it becomes—and is seen and understood to be—the world's premier institution in that activity. Given the increasing clout of private capital markets and its implications for exchange rate management, some have proposed that the Fund increase its surveillance of these markets. Dini (1995) has suggested that the Fund be given authorization to borrow in private capital markets (so as to meet threats of global financial crises).

Turning to governance issues, several commentators (e.g., Finch 1994; Williamson and Henning 1994) feel that the Fund's Executive Board would need to be upgraded (say, by appointing ministerial deputies as executive directors of the Fund), reduced in size, and called together less frequently if the Fund were to become more heavily involved in system management. Creating a subcommittee of the board devoted exclusively to international monetary issues (containing the executive directors of the major industrial countries) is another entry for the suggestion box (Bretton Woods Commission 1994a).

As regards the Interim Committee, some (e.g., Bergsten 1994a) have proposed abolishing it in favor of a newly created council, while others (e.g., Volcker 1994) feel efforts should be made to make its twice yearly meetings of finance ministers more fruitful. Bringing in prominent outside advisers from the private sector either to direct the Fund's forecasting and coordination exercise (to make it less sensitive to political pressures), or to counsel the managing director of the Fund (e.g., to stay abreast better of financial market developments), or to evaluate the need for changes in key-currency exchange rates, also has adherents (Bretton Woods Commission 1994a; Gyohten 1994; Dobson 1994b). Finally, timely publication of IMF country reports has been put forward as a mechanism for increasing the impact of Fund macroeconomic policy advice (Fischer 1994; Dobson 1994b).

Initial Reaction of Policy Authorities

To this point, policy authorities have presented only their initial reactions to the proposals and suggestions mentioned above for reforming or altering the exchange rate system and the policy coordination process. It may be that they will have plans of their own to unveil within the next year. Still, it is fair to say that thus far these authorities have had little difficulty in restraining their enthusiasm for most of the proposals put forward.

Reactions of the G-7

At the July 1994 plenary meeting of the Bretton Woods Commission (1994b), finance deputies from the three key-currency countries—that is, State Treasury Secretary Gert Haller for Germany, Vice Minister Kosuke Nakahira for Japan, and Under Secretary of the Treasury Lawrence Summers for the United States—all expressed the view that "flexible exchange rate bands" (loud target zones) as proposed in the commission's report, or a return to fixed exchange rates, would *not* be helpful to the performance of the world economy.[7]

---

7. This is a long-standing position that has also been held by G-3 central bank officials. Among the rest of the G-7, Canada has long been a strong advocate of managed floating. The position of the United Kingdom has undergone a number of shifts—from a strong advocate of managed floating under the early years of the Thatcher regime, to Chancellor Nigel Lawson's "shadowing" the deutsche mark during the later Thatcher years, to a proponent of the disciplining attributes of explicit exchange rate targets during its stay in

Haller (1994, 21) concluded that "there are both theoretical and practical reasons to refrain from target zones or exchange rate bands." Nakahira (1994, 22) noted that the proposal to set exchange rate bands "seems to involve a variety of practical problems" including political difficulties in setting the ranges, political sensitivities in changing them when economic conditions change, and vulnerabilities of the bands to speculative pressures. And Summers (1994a, 19) cautioned against the serious error implicit "in overly rigid suggestions that because times were more tranquil and exchange rates were more stable in the 1960s, an attempt to construct a more rigid system would bring back the stability that was prevailing in an earlier era." The G-3 deputies prefer instead to try to strengthen the current regime of managed floating and G-7 policy coordination.

In a similar vein, there has been no official support among the G-3 for moving toward more formal coordination rules or guidelines along the lines of the Williamson-Miller (1987) blueprint. Summers (1994b), for example, has maintained that, in a world of proud legislatures and independent central banks, prospects for the implementation of such macroeconomic coordination rules are dim; that such blueprints presume a degree of precision in economic forecasting that is unrealistic; and that such schemes can easily fall prey to the law of unintended consequences.[8] He argues that a widening rather than a deepening of existing G-7 coordination is likely to be the most fruitful, especially if the widening takes the form of increasing cooperation on structural policies and of bringing the larger developing countries into the process.

If proposals for target zones and for a more rule-based approach to policy coordination have not been embraced by the official sector, this does not necessarily mean that the limited menu (floating or monetary unification) offered by the corners school has yet won the day either. In western Europe, where exchange arrangements in the ERM have been in

---

the ERM (1990–92), to a supporter of domestic inflation targets *cum* enough exchange rate flexibility to ensure monetary policy independence (since sterling's exit from the ERM). Historically, France and Italy have been the most enthusiastic among the G-7 about the stability and disciplinary attributes of explicit exchange rate targets *cum* a rule-based international monetary system. Over the past year, however, French and Italian monetary authorities seem to have softened their position on the feasibility and desirability of hard exchange rate commitments among the G-3; see Trichet (1994) and Dini (1994). Official pronouncements aside, some observers (e.g., Bergsten 1994b) have argued that the G-7 has been operating a de facto target zone regime since 1987.

8. Speaking at the same conference, Cooper (1994) likewise regards as politically unsustainable any international coordination rule or scheme that would take away too much authority from national legislatures about tax and expenditure decisions. He characterizes this as one of two fatal weaknesses in the Williamson-Henning blueprint. The other one is that the blueprint requires national current account targets when, according to Cooper (1994), there is no basis for establishing such targets in today's world. And without agreement on current account targets, there can be no agreement on equilibrium exchange rates either. Williamson (1994a) challenges this view.

a state of flux ever since the forced move to wider margins (plus or minus 15 percent) in the summer of 1993, there has been no agreement to declare these wider margins "normal," so as to comply with one of the entry requirements stipulated in the Maastricht Treaty for EMU. Thus, while these countries seem to be in no rush to return to narrow margins—or, in the cases of the United Kingdom and Italy, to even rejoin the ERM— they have yet to be convinced that the only way to make a smooth transition to EMU is to forgo any further attempt to maintain tight exchange rate targets during the transition.

Nor has there exactly been a groundswell of support in the official sector—at least in the industrial countries—for proposals to increase the IMF's role in coordinating macroeconomic policies and in developing and implementing international monetary reforms. To my knowledge, no new concrete proposals on this score have been advanced by any G-3 or G-7 country. The prevailing view among the G-7 (at least prior to the Mexican crisis) seems to have been that the Fund's existing systemic role was adequate and that an effort to cut back the Fund's activities in the developing world in order to have it focus more on overseeing the international monetary system would be unwise. Summers (1994b), for instance, has characterized the IMF's role in supporting stabilization in the developing world and in the economies in transition as the area where the Fund is likely to make the greatest contribution in the next few years.

Reaction of the Fund

As for the reaction of the Fund itself to the various reform proposals, it has staked out a flexible position. Speaking in his personal capacity, the managing director of the Fund has on several recent occasions (Camdessus 1994a, 1994b, 1994c) expressed a "yearning" for a return to pegged exchange rates among the major currencies (because of its positive disciplinary effect on policies and its benign influence on trade and investment). But he has acknowledged that the collective determination necessary to maintain such a system—including the willingness to accept short-run costs in growth and employment when diverting monetary policy from domestic to external objectives—is still absent in the largest industrial countries. As such, he sees the scope for improving the functioning of the system resting in the near term on ongoing efforts to achieve better macroeconomic and structural policies via strengthened IMF surveillance.[9]

The Fund has welcomed calls for it to play a more central systemic role but has cautioned that it can only do what its membership (including its

---

9. IMF staff (Mussa et al. 1994a) have been less equivocal, concluding that fundamental reform of the exchange rate system is likely to be neither practical nor desirable.

main shareholders) authorizes it to do. Pending such authorization, the Fund has not proposed changes in its governance. And rather than retreat from its work on developing countries engaged in stabilization and structural adjustment and reform, Camdessus (1994c) has argued, the Fund "must do even more and do it even better."

3

What Can Be Done?

As the preceding chapters made clear, we are at an impasse on what to do about the exchange rate system. While there is widespread agreement that it would be desirable to reduce the frequency, size, and duration of exchange rate misalignments, there is as yet no meeting of the minds on how to bring that about. Fundamental reform of the exchange rate system and/or of the institutional architecture for international economic policy coordination—in the sense of a move to explicit, binding exchange rate targets by the G-3 countries and a wholesale transfer of responsibility for organizing international economic policy coordination from the G-7 back to the IMF—does not seem to be in the cards. Even if it was, some (myself included) would argue that it would more likely make things worse rather than better. At the same time, it is not clear what modest changes to the system should have priority and what their impact would be if they were in fact implemented.

In the remainder of this study, I outline the rationale for, and the specifics of, a *modest agenda* for improving the functioning of the exchange rate system. In brief, I have looked for the intersection of two sets of proposals: those that stand at least a fighting chance of being accepted by policy authorities in the major industrial countries, and those that, if implemented, would make a helpful (but not a trivial) contribution to the operation of the system.

Short-Run Exchange Rate Variability versus Misalignment

The rationale begins with the proposition that management of the exchange rate system ought to focus on avoiding large and prolonged misalignments, particularly for the key currencies since these have the largest spillover effects on the performance of the global economy. Like the real wage rate and the real interest rate, the real exchange rate is an important relative price. The experience of the past 25 years suggests that large misalignments are costly because they seriously distort resource allocation, because their correction sometimes carries with it disruptive strains in financial markets, and because they can fuel pressures to resort to protectionist or other administrative solutions for dealing with external imbalances.[1]

High short-run variability of nominal and real exchange rates is no doubt a nuisance to traders and investors, but available empirical evidence for industrial countries does not suggest any kind of robust link with economic performance—be it for international trade, investment, or economic growth (see the annex). In the relatively few cases where such a link has been found, the effect of exchange rate variability was small and usually declining over time. The greater availability of instruments for hedging exchange rate risk (swaps, options, forwards, futures) and the increasing weight of multinational corporations with global production facilities probably have contributed to this outcome. Higher short-term exchange rate variability has *not* been a major factor in the observed decline in industrial-country growth rates from those of the golden years of the Bretton Woods period; the slowdown in growth rates reflects primarily a slowdown in productivity growth, and current research has found little reason to suspect that short-run exchange rate variability has much to do with it. There are some hints that higher short-run exchange rate variability may have reduced the sensitivity of industrial-country trade flows to exchange rate changes, that it may have discouraged investment in developing countries, and perhaps that it may have prompted a

---

1. While the literature on the costs of exchange rate misalignments is growing, existing empirical studies are fewer than one might have thought. Several merit explicit mention. Dunn (1973) and Makin (1974) analyze the investment distortions associated with misalignments in the latter years of the Bretton Woods regime. Marston (1988) contains a set of studies on the effects of misalignment, particularly misalignment of the US dollar in the mid-1980s, on trade and industry. Krugman (1991a) and Hooper and Marquez (1993) examine the effect of exchange rates on current and trade account adjustment in the industrial countries. Goldstein et al. (1993) and the Group of Ten (1993) discuss the role of exchange rate expectations in capital inflows to high–interest rate ERM countries during 1990–92, as well as the strains in financial markets that took place during the ERM crisis in the fall of 1992. Edwards (1989) presents evidence that developing countries that have been subject to relatively large real exchange rate misalignments have recorded poorer economic performance than those with smaller misalignments. Grilli (1988) offers some empirical support for the proposition that the demand for protectionist trade policies in the United States and Europe has been greatest during periods of relatively large misalignments. Since the openness of the larger industrial countries is considerably greater than it was two or three decades ago (see IMF 1994; Krugman 1995), there is a strong presumption that misalignments (of a given size) would be more costly today than 20 or 30 years ago—but less costly (for the larger countries themselves) than they would be in smaller, more open economies.

greater international diversification of production facilities (with some loss in economies of scale), but not more than that.

Sources of Misalignment

Misalignments occur under both fixed and floating exchange rate regimes.[2] In fixed rate and adjustable peg systems, misalignments reflect either an inappropriate entry rate or, more often, a tendency for authorities to wait too long in moving the nominal exchange rate to accommodate changes in economic fundamentals.[3] In cases where a binding exchange rate target has been used successfully for some time as a nominal anchor, countries often find it difficult to switch to using the exchange rate as a tool of relative price adjustment even when circumstances and the limitations of other adjustment instruments argue forcefully for such a change. Small, timely changes in exchange rates (within the band) might discourage destabilizing speculation, but history suggests such a "depolitization" of exchange rate adjustments will often be problematic when authorities rather than markets set the rate.[4] Countries still seem to act as if devaluations of fixed rates carry a high political cost for the devaluing country.[5]

In floating rate regimes, misalignments occur because markets move exchange rates too much in relation to fundamentals. But why and how that occurs is still largely an unsettled question. The ability of structural exchange rate models (that incorporate economic fundamentals) to explain or to forecast the time-series behavior of floating exchange rates has thus far proved to be quite limited, at least at short-term time horizons (up to a year or so); only over the longer term do fundamentals seem to assert

---

2. Williamson (1994a) contains a set of studies that both examine the conceptual foundation of equilibrium exchange rates and that provide estimates of misalignments. Estimates of the extent of misalignment for the major currencies during the latter years of Bretton Woods are presented in Bayoumi et al. (1994). Williamson (1994b) presents estimates of misalignment for the major currencies during the floating rate period.

3. For example, some analysts (Wren-Lewis et al. 1991) have argued that sterling entered the ERM in 1990 at too high (appreciated) an exchange rate.

4. I say "might" discourage destabilizing speculation because the outcome is not a foregone conclusion. Fleming (1970) and Obstfeld (1995), for example, argue that there is no way for authorities to credibly commit to making only small changes in the parity.

5. Cooper (1971) provided an early empirical analysis of the political cost of devaluation (in developing countries). Klein and Marion (1994), using logit analysis on a data set of exchange rate pegs for 16 Latin American countries and Jamaica during 1957–91, show that political factors still are significant in determining the likelihood of an exchange rate change. Closer at hand, political factors have been frequently cited as one of the elements inhibiting a more timely adjustment of the Mexican peso (in 1993 or 1994). It is similarly hard to believe that political factors in some EMS countries did not play a part in the difficulty of agreeing on a revaluation of the deutsche mark after German unification.

themselves.[6] This has made it difficult to get much of a picture (from empirical work) of which fundamentals matter most for exchange rates, and by implication, to know much about the sources of misalignment (typically defined as the difference between the actual exchange rate and the rate implied by fundamentals). It has also resulted in only a loose connection between the methods used to define and estimate equilibrium exchange rates and the models used to explain the (short- to medium-term) behavior of actual (floating) exchange rates.[7] Work on the microeconomic structure of the foreign exchange market has been expanding rapidly in recent years but is still at too early a stage to yield concrete policy recommendations (Frankel and Rose 1995). All this has reduced the confidence authorities (in floating-rate countries) have in all estimates of misalignments. In any case, they often seem reluctant to second-guess the market even when the exchange rate moves to levels that are hard to explain on the basis of their own perceptions of fundamentals.

Key Shortcoming of the Present System

A key shortcoming of present arrangements is thus that exchange rate decisions (and/or associated macroeconomic policy adjustments) are

---

6. Frankel and Rose (1995) provide a comprehensive survey of recent empirical research on the determination and behavior of nominal exchange rates. At short time horizons (up to one year), researchers have found that structural models of floating exchange rates (based on macroeconomic fundamentals) have been unable to outperform (i.e., forecast out of sample) "naive" models, even when the structural models were provided with ex post information on future fundamentals such as money and output (see Meese and Rogoff 1983a and 1983b and later work summarized in Frankel and Rose 1995). At medium-term and longer horizons, fundamentals seem to do better, although even here, little is yet resolved as to which fundamentals count most, how best to measure those fundamentals, and how the microeconomics of the foreign exchange market affects the weight given to economic fundamentals at different points in time (Obstfeld 1995; Flood and Rose 1993; Frankel and Rose 1995). Mussa (1990) offers some possible explanations for why empirical models of floating exchange rates based on (monetary) fundamentals have had such difficulty in explaining the observed behavior of floating exchange rates.

7. As discussed in IMF (1984b), Williamson (1985, 1994b), Frenkel and Goldstein (1988), Clark et al. (1994), and Stein (1994), there are various methods of defining and estimating equilibrium exchange rates. Much of the work seems to have followed on Nurkse (1945), who defined the equilibrium rate as the exchange rate that would produce equilibrium in the balance of payments— when there was no excessive unemployment, no undue restrictions on trade, and no special incentives to incoming or outgoing capital flows. Williamson (1994b) and Clark et al. (1994) define the equilibrium exchange rate as the exchange rate that is consistent with the simultaneous achievement of internal and external balance (in the medium term). Stein (1994) defines it as the rate that would prevail if cyclical and speculative factors could be removed while unemployment is at its natural rate. Other approaches include departures from purchasing power parity based on choice of an equilibrium base year (McKinnon and Ohno 1988) and the sustainability of debt ratios implied by the current account implications of the market's forecast of the future exchange rate (Krugman 1985). While some of the variables highlighted in these equilibrium calculations appear in models trying to explain the behavior of actual exchange rates, the connection is loose at best.

delayed for too long, with the result that large misalignments occur more frequently and last longer than they should. Although the major industrial countries usually claim that they can overcome this problem by their own efforts, their track record argues otherwise. A more politically independent, outside overseer of the system that specializes in the monitoring and evaluation of exchange rate misalignments ought to be able to help "tilt" countries in the direction of making these crucial exchange rate (and macroeconomic policy) decisions on a more timely basis; a proposal to this effect will be detailed below.

It is generally believed that large misalignments are more likely to take place when the policy fundamentals are poor than when they are sound.[8] Stronger economic policy fundamentals should therefore help to reduce misalignments. But the capacity of the exchange rate regime to deliver improvements in fundamentals differs across policies and countries. Binding exchange rate targets have greater potential to discipline monetary policy than fiscal policy. Yet the three key-currency countries—whose exchange rate policies form the nucleus of the exchange rate system— have less incentive than others to use the exchange rate regime for that purpose. Each of the G-3 has demonstrated relatively good inflation performance over the past decade without the aid of binding exchange rate targets, their central banks are among the most independent in the world, and the tendency toward greater symmetry in economic influence among them makes the choice of a single anchor country problematic.[9] Moreover, the expected pattern of shocks across these three countries is dissimilar enough to make them wary of forsaking monetary policy independence, and their structural characteristics (size, openness, etc.) make them less sensitive to large exchange rate fluctuations than their smaller neighbors.

In contrast, the key-currency countries (and particularly the United States) have recorded some notable lapses in fiscal policy discipline over the past decade. Mechanisms that would "tie their hands" on fiscal policy

---

8. Interestingly enough, I don't believe this proposition has been subject to much formal empirical testing.

9. Goldstein and Isard (1992) examine the inflation performance of 23 industrial countries over the 1954–90 period. Germany's record (measured using consumer prices) is the best over the period as a whole, and it consistently ranked in the top three in the 1960s, 1970s, and 1980s. Japan recorded the best inflation performance (using either consumer or wholesale prices) among the 23 countries in the 1980s, and the second lowest average rate of wholesale price inflation for the period as a whole. The United States ranked seventh for the period as a whole and has done much to rebuild its anti-inflationary credibility since the early 1980s.

Obstfeld (1995) finds that for most G-10 countries, there is no striking rise in the persistence of national inflation rates for the post-1973 period as a whole. Goldstein and Isard (1992) document the decline in the relative economic size of the United States vis-à-vis Europe and Japan over the past 30 years. According to the index of Alesina and Summers (1991), the Bundesbank is the most independent of industrial-country central banks; the US Federal Reserve ranks third of 15 industrial countries, while the Bank of Japan ranks sixth.

therefore have some attraction. But the exchange rate regime is too indirect and faulty a filter to constrain fiscal policy effectively. For example, an exchange rate rule can call for monetization of an excessive fiscal deficit rather than for correction of the fiscal deficit itself (Frenkel and Goldstein 1986). In the historical cases where fiscal policy in the key-currency countries has gone furthest off the track, it is doubtful that binding exchange rate targets would have prevented these policy errors. More generally, there appears to be little connection between the exchange rate regime and the extent of fiscal policy discipline (Obstfeld 1995).

Simulation exercises with multicountry macroeconomic models typically show that if exchange rate targets in the G-3 countries had been more binding on policy than they actually were (via either fixed exchange rates or loud target zones), it is likely that economic performance would have been worse than it was—not better. The most comprehensive exercise of that type is the one conducted by Bryant et al. (1993), which collected the results from eight well-known multicountry econometric models, ran stochastic as well as deterministic simulations, and compared four alternative policy regimes for monetary policy.[10] One of the authors' main conclusions bears explicit mention:

> Either nominal-income targeting or real-GNP-plus-inflation targeting, in contrast to money targeting or exchange rate targeting, best stabilizes national economies if the loss functions of policymakers stress real ultimate target variables such as output or employment, or if the loss function stresses a combination of such real variables and nominal ultimate target variables such as the rate of inflation or the price level. (Bryant et al. 1993, 30)[11]

For the foreseeable future, the largest industrial countries are likely to seek greater fiscal discipline via mechanisms outside the exchange rate regime—both national (balanced budget amendments and the like) and international (G-7 policy coordination). It is likewise noteworthy that when the Maastricht Treaty was agreed, it was decided not to rely on maintenance of exchange rates within regular margins (over the two years previous to entry into Economic and Monetary Union) as a sufficient guarantee that fiscal convergence would be appropriate; instead, separate entry criteria were included for fiscal deficits and stocks of government debt relative to GNP (see Kenen 1992).

---

10. Nevertheless, because Bryant et al. (1993) looked only at alternative monetary policy regimes and did not consider alternative fiscal policy regimes, some supporters of exchange rate targeting may regard their conclusions as less than fully convincing.

11. In order to get exchange rate targeting to be the winning monetary policy regime for the G-3 in such simulations, one has to assume either that the variability of exchange rates and/or interest rates should be included in the loss function, or that the future would be characterized by the preponderance of a particular kind of shock that is best handled by fixed rates. Neither such assumption seems warranted.

Credible and Consistent Exchange Rate Policy for the G-3

What then should the exchange rate policy of the three key-currency countries be? The G-3 countries should pledge to monitor exchange rate developments closely and be willing both to engage in concerted intervention and to alter the course of monetary policy away from domestic priorities in those (unusual) circumstances when, by common consent, there is a large misalignment of their currencies. The guiding principle behind this policy is that no more should be promised on exchange rate policy than can credibly be delivered.

Such an exchange rate policy offers five advantages. First and most important, it is credible because it is consistent with the two key facts of life about monetary policy and exchange rate policy in these countries: monetary policy is the only policy instrument that is likely to be effective in managing exchange rates under conditions of strong market pressures, and G-3 monetary policy authorities will almost always choose domestic objectives when they conflict with exchange rate objectives.

Consider the potential policy instruments for managing exchange rates. Fiscal policy is too inflexible an instrument (particularly now that most industrial countries face medium-term or long-term problems with public-sector deficits and/or debt ratios), and its effect on exchange rates too uncertain (even in direction), to be handed the task of exchange rate management. Moreover, fiscal policy is one of the most difficult policy instruments to coordinate internationally (Tanzi 1988).

Sterilized exchange-market intervention is fine for smoothing disorderly markets and maybe even for influencing exchange rates (at least in the short term) when markets do not have clear view of their own. But it is no substitute for monetary policy action when markets hold a concerted view different from that of authorities.[12] Recent research on the effectiveness of sterilized intervention is consistent with this view.[13] Recall that the one of the main conclusions of the Jurgensen Report (1983) was that while sterilized intervention might have some short-run impact on exchange rates, it did not appear to have much long-run impact, and its effects were often swamped by those of other macroeconomic policies (Jurgensen 1983; Edison 1993). Recent evidence supplements that with the additional conclusions that sterilized intervention is likely to be more effective both when it is announced (versus being kept quiet) and

---

12. When capital flows become very large, the ability to sterilize these flows also comes under strain. See Goldstein et al. (1993) for a treatment of the strains put on the Bundesbank's monetary management by its very large intervention operations during the 1992 ERM crisis.

13. See Edison (1993) for a survey of recent work on the effectiveness of sterilized central-bank intervention. Obstfeld (1990, 1995) also appraises the experience with sterilized intervention in the late 1980s and early 1990s.

when it is coordinated across countries (versus being undertaken on a unilateral basis).[14] Recent research also suggests that when sterilized intervention does have an impact on exchange rates, it is likely to operate more through the "signaling" channel than through the "portfolio balance" channel—that is, more by affecting market participants' expectations about the future exchange rate than by altering the stocks of relative asset supplies and the risk premium. But there is little in recent research to warrant embracing the revisionist view that sterilized intervention has a long-lasting, significant effect on exchange rates, or that it can reverse market trends, or that it can extract the authorities from serious internal-external policy dilemmas.[15]

Meanwhile, the heyday of capital controls has long since passed. Enhanced possibilities for switching across financial products and geo-

---

14. Dominguez and Frankel (1993) furnish evidence on both these points.

15. Edison (1993) and Obstfeld (1995) reach similar conclusions. Perhaps the most discussed challenge to this view is the study by Catte, Galli, and Rebecchini (1994). They examine the relationship between G-3 exchange rates and sterilized intervention over 1985–91, drawing on daily data of the intervention activities of 16 central banks. They subdivide the period into 19 episodes in which intervention was coordinated among at least two of the three major countries. Graphical techniques are used throughout; no regressions are run. Three of their more striking conclusions are that all of the episodes were successful in the sense that intervention inverted the trend of the dollar; that in 9 of the 19 episodes, intervention was definitely successful in the sense that the next intervention episode was in the opposite direction; and that all but one of the major turning points of the dollar coincided exactly with episodes of concerted intervention.

Truman (1994), Mussa et al. (1994b), and Obstfeld (1995), among others, have commented on the Catte, Galli, and Rebecchini study, and each reached the conclusion that the inferences drawn by the authors from their tests *overstate* considerably the effectiveness of intervention. I fully share that conclusion. Movements of the yen/dollar and deutsche mark/dollar exchange rate at high frequencies (daily, weekly, etc.) are known not to display persistent trends. Instead, they approximate a random walk. Thus, even if completely ineffective intervention were imposed on this pattern of exchange rate movements, one would expect to see a significant percentage of back-and-forth movements and reversals. The hypothesis that intervention is ineffective and authorities cease doing it when, by chance, exchange rates eventually reverse course is therefore as consistent with the data as the hypothesis that intervention is very effective. Moreover, because only graphical techniques are employed, it is not possible to control for the simultaneity between exchange rates and intervention, thus clouding what causes what. Their results are also likely to be sensitive to the length of the period for each episode (which is arbitrary). Truman (1994) reckons that, according to his personal judgmental criteria, intervention was partially successful in 5 of the 19 episodes. Obstfeld (1995) also applies the same graphical technique to later episodes of sterilized intervention in 1993–95 and reports no consistent pattern of effectiveness.

Dominguez and Frankel (1993) also use daily data to test the effectiveness of sterilized intervention, in this case on the dollar/deutsche mark exchange rate over 1982–90. This study uses regression techniques and is not subject to the methodological pitfalls present in the Catte, Galli, and Rebecchini study . Dominguez and Frankel conclude that sterilized intervention is more effective when it is announced and concerted than when it is not. They also conclude that it is more potent than the Jurgensen Report or most officials claim it to be—without going so far as to suggest that it has achieved "success ratios" anything like those claimed by Catte, Galli, and Rebecchini.

graphic areas make all but the most wide-ranging controls or taxes ineffective, and comprehensive controls risk discouraging what some authorities
might regard as "good" capital flows (trade credit, hedging operations)
along with "bad" ones.[16] The past decade has also witnessed a trend in
the industrial countries toward rising nonresident ownership of a large
and increasing stock of government debt; the share held by nonresidents
of the public debt of the G-7 countries now exceeds 20 percent (Goldstein
et al. 1994). In effect, these governments came to the decision that if their
growing debt was to be sold at low cost, they would have to tap the
international market and simultaneously reform their government securities markets so as to be attractive to international institutional investors.[17]
The point is that after having undergone these reforms—most of them
aimed at increasing liquidity and transparency—they are likely to be
wary of measures that would reduce liquidity and risk alienating (possibly
over the longer term) the very professional investors that they have
worked so hard to attract. Nor is the available empirical evidence on the
effect of security transactions taxes kind to the view that these taxes
reduce volatility.[18]

In sum, this means that, if only by default, **the task of exchange rate
management has to fall to monetary policy**. Yet any assignment rule
that assumes that exchange rate management is the primary objective of
G-3 central banks will lack credibility, since market participants have
already learned from experience that when push comes to shove the
interest rate adjustments needed to defend ambitious exchange rate commitments will not be forthcoming. Only when exchange rate misalignments are judged to be large and serious will the monetary authorities be
willing to sacrifice domestic objectives to eliminate those misalignments.

A second advantage of the exchange rate policy outlined above is that,
by specifying that only potentially "large" misalignments will bring forth
intervention and monetary policy action, it recognizes another reality: in
the current state of the art, all estimates of equilibrium exchange rates

---

16. Garber and Taylor (1995) provide a persuasive analysis of how sand-in-the-wheels taxes
and similar impediments are likely to be evaded in today's global capital markets. Recall
as well that none of the three countries (Spain, Portugal, and Ireland) that imposed controls
or tightened existing regulations during the ERM crisis of 1992 was able to avoid a devaluation, and each removed them within a few months' time. Mathieson and Rojas-Suarez (1993),
after studying the experience of both industrial and developing countries with capital
controls over the past two decades, conclude that the effectiveness of controls has declined
over time because the transactions costs of moving funds have decreased while the incentives
for doing so have increased.

17. Most of these reforms of government securities markets are patterned on the standards
established in the US government securities markets. Goldstein et al. (1994) describe the
nature of these reforms in the G-10 countries.

18. See Hakkio (1994) for a review of this experience with security transaction taxes and
stock market price limits.

are subject to a substantial margin of error.[19] This means that it will be much harder to elicit enough support for concerted action when estimated misalignments are small (say, less than 10 percent) than when they are larger. The main conceptual problem is that optimal current account positions are subject to a considerable range of indeterminacy for most industrial countries (in most circumstances, a deficit equal, say, to 1 percent of GNP is just as plausible as a 1 percent surplus).[20] Yet precise estimates of those optimal or desired current account positions are needed to drive precise estimates of equilibrium exchange rates. This range of uncertainty about equilibrium exchange rates need not—and should not—cripple exchange rate management if authorities leave enough leeway to accommodate it.

Third, by relying on markets to make judgments on exchange rates most of the time and by invoking the escape clause only in unusual circumstances, this policy reduces (but does not eliminate) the danger that needed exchange rate adjustments will be too long delayed because of their political ramifications or because there is no agreement among authorities on the right rate. The inability of ERM participants to agree in 1990–91 on an orderly appreciation of the deutsche mark to accommodate the fiscal effects of German unification testifies to the relevance of timely decision making for avoiding a crisis. Markets may at times move exchange rates by too much or too little, but they are not subject to destabilizing inaction.

Fourth, by not committing the authorities to defend a preannounced parity or target range, this policy is much less susceptible to successful speculative attacks that push authorities into an undefensible position, sometimes at considerable public-sector cost. Another major lesson from the ERM crises of 1992 and 1993 is that there are periods when the benefit-cost calculus of speculative attacks very much favors the attacker rather than the defender of fixed rates. The attackers have been buoyed, inter alia, by the increasing financial muscle of institutional investors, some of whom have great flexibility in their risk-taking strategies (hedge funds alone now have about $75 billion to $100 billion of capital); by the growing range of large players (financial and nonfinancial) who have significant access to foreign exchange; by secular declines in the transactions costs associated with switching the currency denomination of portfolios; and by an increased range of instruments offering high-leverage ratios.[21]

---

19. Williamson (1994b) compares estimates of equilibrium exchange rates for the major currencies generated by six multicountry econometric models. The range of estimates for each currency was wide.

20. Clark et al. (1994) also discuss other tough nuts that have to be cracked to estimate equilibrium exchange rates.

21. Eichengreen (1994) and Obstfeld (1995) also argue that the defenders have been weakened (relative, say, to their position under the gold standard) by the greater political influence of labor and the greater accountability of politicians for economic downturns.

Meanwhile, prospects for a successful interest rate defense of fixed parities have been shown to be dim when the defending country suffers from either fragility in the financial sector, or weak fiscal fundamentals *cum* high shares of short-term and floating-rate government debt, or high debt ratios in the household and corporate sectors, or high unemployment. In those circumstances, trying to "squeeze" the speculators by radically increasing their cost of funds (overnight interest rates of 500 percent or so) is not credible because such action simultaneously carries a prohibitive domestic cost. Goldstein et al. (1993, 15) explain the nature of this kind of interest rate vulnerability from the perspective of the 1992 ERM crisis as follows:

> First, the same increase in interest rates that serves to squeeze speculators can simultaneously squeeze the funding of securities and banking markets which typically finance their positions through short-term rollover credit. Since central banks also carry the responsibility for maintaining the safety and soundness of the financial markets, they have to be careful about inducing an extreme punitive rise in central bank lending rates, except perhaps over the very short term.
>
> If some large banks are already laboring under heavy loan losses—or even worse, are on the brink of needing government assistance to remain solvent, rises in interest rates exacerbate their problems and may increase the fiscal deficit (if explicit or implicit government insurance of commercial bank liabilities is present).
>
> Second, in situations where the household and corporate sectors have allowed their debt-to-income and debt-servicing positions to become unsustainably high, a sharp rise in interest rates makes it more difficult to reduce those ratios to more manageable levels—without simultaneously reducing spending to such a large degree as to slow economic activity appreciably. Where the economy is already in recession, the problem takes on an added dimension because of the risk that a protracted period of high interest rates could force the pace of disinflation to become too rapid, and perhaps even push the economy into a debt-deflation cycle.
>
> Third, in countries with both extremely weak fiscal fundamentals, and a large share of short-term and floating-rate government debt, a large increase in interest rates can feed back quickly and powerfully to increase the government's fiscal deficit. At some point, increases in interest rates may actually weaken the attractiveness of the domestic currency if market participants believe that they increase debt-servicing problems or if interest volatility presents asset holders with unacceptably high levels of market risk.
>
> Fourth, high interest rates—maintained mainly to defend an exchange rate target—will often be viewed as having a high opportunity cost in terms of domestic economic activity, particularly where the economy has been in recession, where unemployment rates are high, where inflationary pressures are moderate and receding, and where the consensus forecast is for slow growth in the period ahead. The greater the current differences are between the domestic and external requirements for monetary policy in the weak-currency country, the more likely it is that questions will be raised about the wisdom of "tying one's hands" on monetary policy—whatever the long-term benefits of such a policy strategy.

On top of this, the interest rate increase may not have the intended effect on either speculators or the exchange rate. For example, if short sellers of the domestic currency obtain their financing before the defensive increase in interest rates takes effect, they will not be squeezed by a short-lived increase in interest rates. Even worse, in some dynamic hedging strategies, a rise in the spread between the defending currency's interest rate and interest rates abroad actually mandates a *sale* of the defending currency (Garber and Spencer 1995).

These considerations do not mean, of course, that aggressive interest rate defenses of exchange rate targets cannot work. Rather, they suggest that such a strategy will be difficult to implement successfully in those situations when the defending country has weak (secondary) fundamentals and/or large disparities between the internal and external requirements of monetary policy. The rub is that speculators will not choose the currencies and timing of their attacks randomly: instead, they will attack where and when the vulnerabilities are relatively greatest.[22] As Obstfeld (1995) has aptly put it, they will look for situations where the cost of "hanging on" is large relative to the cost of reneging on the exchange rate commitment.

In addition, the ERM crisis of 1992 also illustrated that speculative attacks have other dynamic elements. Specifically, a country that had no need for an exchange rate adjustment can find its competitive position weakened, and its susceptibility to attack increased, once several of its key trading partners have devalued their currencies in response to an attack.

This increased clout and agility of private capital markets is here to stay.[23] If exchange rate policy is to be viable, the authorities have to pick carefully their spots to go against the markets—not issue an open invitation to play table stakes poker with an opponent who has a much larger pile of chips and a much less binding set of operating constraints.

The fifth advantage of the proposed exchange rate policy is that, by restricting challenges to the market to cases where there is by "common consent" an emerging large misalignment, this policy acknowledges that go-it-alone exchange rate policy is increasingly ineffective. Yet another lesson of the ERM crisis is that when the burden of interest rate adjustment is not shared relatively symmetrically between the weak- and strong-currency countries during an attack—because, say, the strong-currency country regards the domestic requirements of monetary policy as superseding the external ones—prospects for success are very much dimin-

---

22. In this connection, Goldstein et al. (1993) note that prior to the 1992 ERM crisis Sweden had a large fiscal deficit and significant financial fragility; the United Kingdom had experienced two years of recession, had excessive debt accumulation in the private sector, and had a financial market structure in which any rise in the Bank of England's minimum dealing rate spread relatively quickly to the whole yield curve (including retail and mortgage markets); and Italy had a size and structure of its government debt under which increases in interest rates had relatively large adverse feedback effects on government finance.

23. Goldstein and Mussa (1994) provide an analysis of how far the integration of national capital markets has proceeded, along with an evaluation of the clout of these markets in disciplining government policies.

ished. For in that case, the weak-currency country has to increase its domestic interest rate by an unsustainably large amount. Likewise, the aforementioned recent empirical work on sterilized intervention suggests that concerted intervention generally has a larger impact than the unilateral variety. One reason the authorities were better able to defend the French franc than some other ERM rates (sterling, the peseta, the escudo) in the fall of 1992 was that the Bundesbank made it much clearer in the former case that speculators would be fighting against two central banks rather than one. In a similar vein, had the G-3 countries implemented coordinated interest rate action in, say, March 1995, I believe they would have sent a much stronger signal to the foreign exchange market than was conveyed by the unilateral interest rate cuts of both the Bundesbank and the Bank of Japan.

But if the authorities keep their estimates of the equilibrium exchange rate (or target zone) quiet, won't they give up the stabilizing forces that come into play when market participants believe that authorities will intervene to keep actual rates close to equilibrium ones (or at least within the target zone)? To be sure, the last seven years or so have seen the development of a class of theoretical models of target zones that demonstrate rigorously what previously had only been intuitive—namely, that if market participants have confidence that announced exchange rate targets will be defended, these targets or zones will be inherently stabilizing.[24]

The $64,000 question is whether market participants will in fact have "confidence" that these exchange rate targets will be defended. For the kind of "soft" exchange rate commitments laid out earlier as part of the modest agenda, I think little stabilizing speculation is likely to be generated (particularly over the first few years of operation) whether the zones are loud or quiet; hence, little is to be sacrificed by keeping them quiet. I come to that conclusion in part because empirical evidence of a "honeymoon effect" for exchange rate schemes that carried much harder commitments and had much more at stake than those outlined above (e.g., the ERM) is quite limited.[25] Most of these tests have been carried out only over the past few years. The original assumptions of the Krugman (1991) target zone model (namely, that the target zone is perfectly credible and that the zones are defended only by marginal interventions) have been consistently rejected by the data (Garber and Svensson 1995). So too have been the implications of the original model for the behavior of exchange rates within target zones.[26] More recently, researchers have been able to

---

24. Much of this literature has been driven by the target zone models developed by Krugman (1987b, 1991b). Reviews of that literature are contained in Garber and Svensson (1995) and Svensson (1992).

25. See, for example, Frankel and Phillips (1992) on ERM credibility.

26. The most important of those implications are that there should be a nonlinear (S-shaped) relationship between the exchange rate and fundamentals, that the exchange rate should spend most of its time near the edges of the band, and that there should be a negative

generate predictions that accord better with the data by varying the original model to permit intramarginal intervention and time-varying realignment risk. This allows some retention of honeymoon effects but at the cost both of removing some of the strong testable assumptions of the original model and of transforming a target zone model into a model of managed floating (*cum* frequent intramarginal intervention; see Garber and Svensson 1995).

Only when authorities have maintained a hard exchange rate commitment over a long period and when the country has relatively small longer-term incentives to seek monetary policy independence—as, for example, in the case of the Dutch guilder—are strong stabilizing expectations likely to come into play. Getting it on the cheap for the G-3 countries seems a dubious proposition. What is more plausible is that a consistent application of the exchange rate policy outlined above could at least convince market participants that someone "is minding the store" on exchange rate misalignments—that is, monitoring the situation closely and being willing to take forceful, concerted actions when those misalignments threaten to become very large. Over time, this could help to deter destabilizing speculation.

There is another reason for not announcing a target zone. It is to be expected that disagreements will arise from time to time among participants about the equilibrium exchange rate. Such disagreements will be easier to reconcile, and less disruptive of markets, when they are not exacerbated by the need to publish target zones.

A final potential objection: Isn't the exchange rate policy outlined above pretty much the same exchange rate policy that the G-3 countries have been following for the last five years or so? Yes and no. Yes, these countries have been following a policy of managed floating without explicit and binding exchange rate commitments. Yes, they have on occasion been willing to engage in coordinated intervention and to indicate that market rates have in their view strayed too far from fundamentals.[27] Even more occasionally, there has been some coordinated interest rate action. But no, the exchange rate policy recommended here would not be the same policy followed heretofore. This is where the IMF and the rest of the modest agenda come in.

A Better Early Warning System

As argued earlier, there ought to be a way to identify emerging misalignments and to take corrective action—be it by changing underlying policies

---

relationship between the exchange rate and the interest differential. See Garber and Svensson (1995) for a review of these empirical results.

27. Catte, Galli, and Rebecchini (1994) report that almost all G-3 interventions over 1985–91 took place during episodes of coordinated intervention.

or adjusting nominal exchange rates—*at an earlier stage*. By the time the G-5 countries were willing to acknowledge publicly at the Plaza Agreement in September 1985 that "some orderly appreciation of nondollar currencies is desirable," the dollar was, by Williamson's (1994b) most recent estimate, already overvalued by roughly 45 percent. To be sure, medium-term swings in real exchange rates of key currencies have been much more moderate since then, and there have no misalignments nearly as large as the 1984–85 dollar. Still, the misalignment of a group of ERM currencies in the early 1990s, and the misalignment of the yen in the late 1980s, suggest that the problem has not gone away.[28] The overvaluations of the Mexican peso and the CFA franc (prior to recent adjustments) likewise forcefully demonstrate that the problem of timely correction is if anything more serious in developing countries than in industrial ones.

If misalignments are to be identified earlier, some institution will have to make that task a key continuing aspect of its operations. In that connection, it is questionable whether the G-7 countries on their own, or regional exchange arrangements like the ERM, can easily overcome their past reticence to challenge either each other or the market. An outside agent that has more political independence and that can supply a more consistent focus to the monitoring and evaluation of exchange rate developments than governments should take on more of that responsibility.[29] The institution best suited to do that is the IMF. More specifically, two complementary sets of concrete steps are needed.

The Role of the IMF

First, the Fund has to upgrade its own monitoring and analysis of key exchange rate developments so that it is better prepared to offer a "view" on misalignments in real time. For this purpose, it ought to have on hand its own estimates of real equilibrium exchange rates—imprecise as they may be—along with other indicators relevant to assessing misalignments and exchange market pressures.[30] Since it almost never makes sense to

---

28. Bergsten and Henning (1995) argue that each of the G-7 currencies has experienced at least one serious misalignment over the past decade.

29. The argument does not require that the IMF be completely politically independent nor that it be able to identify and correct large misalignments with unfailing accuracy. Clearly, it could satisfy neither of those two conditions. The argument simply requires that, on both these counts, performance be better *with* the Fund's active involvement than without it.

30. In addition to the usual macroeconomic fundamentals, estimates of equilibrium exchange rates, and possible indicators of the expected future course of exchange rates (e.g., interest rate differentials, survey data on exchange rate expectations, etc.), it would be useful to look at two sets of factors highlighted by recent exchange market crises. One (relevant mostly for countries with explicit, binding exchange rate targets) is the set of factors that will affect the ability of the country to sustain a period of high interest rates if it is attacked: for example, the fragility of the financial sector, the feedback effects of high interest rates

discuss exchange rate developments in isolation of macroeconomic policies and conditions affecting interest rates and exchange rates, the Fund would of course also need to be prepared to offer its view on how monetary, fiscal, and—occasionally—even structural policies should be conducted over the medium term. And it has to be willing to put its view on exchange rates (and accompanying policies) forward to authorities even when they have not asked for it—something it has not done consistently enough in the past.

Given the increasing clout of private capital markets and the rapidity with which large institutional investors can alter the currency composition of their portfolios in response to "news," the Fund should also increase the frequency and depth of its contacts with those markets so that it has a more timely picture of the current market concerns. Currently, the Fund once a year sends an international capital markets mission to the more important financial centers in North America, Europe, and Asia. The mission discusses capital market developments with monetary and regulatory authorities, commercial and investment banks, securities houses, institutional investors, and stock and futures exchanges. Annual visits are probably no longer sufficient to get a timely view of emerging market concerns.[31] Perhaps the annual mission should be supplemented with short interim visits (say, every quarter or four months) to the three or four main financial centers. Officials spend a lot of time listening and talking to each other. Listening somewhat more to the private markets wouldn't hurt.

Complementary Steps by the G-7

Second, and just as important, the major industrial countries need to give the Fund the opportunity to have its "view" on exchange rates (and on accompanying policies) heard in the forums and at the time when exchange rate and intervention decisions are made. At present, the IMF managing director participates in that part of G-7 policy coordination meetings dealing with surveillance; the economic counsellor of the Fund plays the same role in the meetings of G-7 deputies. But some (perhaps most) of the discussion of exchange rate developments—and all the dis-

---

on the government's fiscal position, and the level and recent trend in unemployment (see also the discussion later in this section). The second set of factors is those that perhaps give some indication (beyond that reflected in interest rate spreads) that creditors are losing confidence in the country's securities: for example, an abrupt shortening in the maturity structure of government debt, or increased use of foreign-currency denominated or foreign-currency indexed debt.

31. The Fund for some time has conducted short, interim visits to G-7 countries between annual Article IV consultations. It is my understanding that proposals are also under discussion (in the aftermath of the Mexican crisis) for the Fund to increase the frequency of its surveillance of member countries that recently emerged from Fund programs.

cussion on intervention strategy—takes place outside the surveillance part of the meeting (when the Fund is not there). Currently, there is no Fund participation at all in key ERM meetings dealing with exchange rates—such as those of the EC Monetary Committee and of the Committee of Central Bank Governors. IMF views on ERM exchange rates are conveyed through more informal channels, or bilaterally at the time of IMF Article IV consultations.

These arrangements are not helpful to serious oversight of the exchange rate system. While the major countries may argue that IMF "approval" of exchange rate decisions would be too constraining and cumbersome, there is much less justification for not hearing its view on exchange rates and related policies in those very meetings where the responsible senior officials debate these policies. Given the capacity of exchange rates to change by large amounts in relatively short periods, a view that is three or six months old (conveyed, say, at the time of the last Fund consultation) will not carry much weight. It is not in the system's interest for regional surveillance of exchange rates (as in the EMS) to supersede global surveillance, especially when four of the world's seven major currencies are involved. Confidentiality would not be compromised by having a senior IMF official participate regularly in these meetings. If an institution is assigned with the task of overseeing the functioning of the exchange rate system, then the major shareholders of that institution ought to facilitate that oversight by inviting the Fund to participate fully in all relevant multilateral meetings on exchange rate and intervention policy.

The most reliable way to implement this suggestion would be to regularize the process. **Specifically, a portion of each G-7 and ERM meeting (at both the ministerial and deputy levels) should be allocated to the discussion of the IMF representative's presentation on exchange rate and macroeconomic developments, including the identification of any potentially serious misalignments for currencies with systemic importance, and the IMF's policy recommendations for dealing with the problem.**[32] Some of this already goes on in the surveillance portion of G-7 meetings—but not consistently enough, not with enough emphasis and attention to identification of emerging exchange rate misalignments, and not with all the analytical focus that the exercise merits.[33] As noted earlier, no such IMF presentation takes place at all in relevant ERM meetings.

---

32. Although G-7 meetings do not have a regular, fixed time schedule, they normally take place frequently enough to provide a timely review of economic developments. Nevertheless, exchange market pressures can develop and come to a head quickly. For that reason, the G-7 should also grant the Fund the authority to convene an emergency meeting of the G-7 in the unlikely event that a potentially serious misalignment is emerging and the G-7 itself has not called a meeting to discuss it. In all other circumstances, the G-7 should continue to set the timing of its meetings.

33. Dobson (1991) gives a full account of the G-7 surveillance exercise, including a description of the Fund's assistance to it.

The case for regularity in exchange rate surveillance is particularly compelling for floating exchange rates. With fixed rates, the authorities are apt to hear an alarm bell when the exchange rate starts to approach either edge of the band. But with floating rates, there is no unique threshold that requires an appraisal of the appropriateness of the market rate.[34] The authorities should therefore supply their own alarm system by both regularizing such appraisals and making the Fund responsible (in the first instance) for sounding the alarm.

The objective of increased Fund participation is not to find something for the Fund to do on industrial-country exchange rate policy: if misalignments could be reduced in frequency and in severity just as easily without its assistance, then it would be better to allocate Fund resources to other tasks. Instead, the point is to use the Fund as an institutional mechanism for reducing the factors that have in the past delayed timely identification and elimination of large exchange rate misalignments.

For this mechanism to work, the Fund has to know that its major shareholders not only encourage it to take on this task but also that they hold it "accountable" for doing that task well. Since it is countries—not the Fund—that ultimately make the final decisions on exchange rate matters, "doing the task well" cannot be judged solely by a before-after comparison of misalignments: for example, if countries ignored the advice of the Fund, large misalignments might occur just as frequently as before. Rather, the litmus test of such a mechanism would be whether the Fund had "blown the whistle" to authorities on emerging exchange rate misalignments when, with the benefit of hindsight, it should have done so. If after a suitable period of observation the Fund does not prove up to that task, it ought to be allocated to some other agency.

Over the longer term, the best hope for greater exchange rate stability lies in inducing the major countries to consistently maintain low inflation rates and prudent fiscal policies, since these will have much to do with establishing a long-term anchor for exchange rate expectations. To the extent that institutional reforms can further these longer-term monetary and fiscal objectives, they are apt to be of a type that falls more in the national than in the international domain (independent central banks with low inflation mandates and constitutional restraints on persistent fiscal deficits). Nevertheless, "international" influences can help to reinforce sound behavior on fundamentals by increasing market and peer pressures on countries to adopt better policies. Again, I believe these are areas where the IMF can make a larger, positive contribution than heretofore.

Making Private Capital Markets Smarter

One constructive step would be for the Fund to use its influence to improve not only the timeliness, regularity, and transparency of country data

---

34. Movements in equity prices and/or interest rate spreads of course provide market signals but, again, do not present an obvious threshold for exchange rate reassessment.

that members submit to it but also the data that they publish for the marketplace—be it in the IMF's *International Financial Statistics* and other Fund publications and/or in the member country's national publications. This is particularly important for variables that matter a lot for assessing exchange rates and interest rates (e.g., international reserves, credit and budgetary policies, external debt). Markets cannot price risk appropriately without timely access to the right information. The poorer the quality of published data on countries' economic situations, the greater is the scope for rumors to exercise undue influence on asset prices. This issue is of particular salience for many developing countries, where the availability and timeliness of published information on economic developments is as yet much more limited than for industrial countries.

Fund member countries already have accepted the obligation to furnish certain types of data in as detailed and accurate a manner as is practical.[35] The Fund, in requesting information, is likewise obligated to take into consideration the varying ability of members to furnish the data requested.[36] Nevertheless, there would seem to be scope for the Fund to take a somewhat firmer stand on the submission and publication of data. Specifically, the Fund and its membership need to reach an understanding that *undue* delays in the reporting of basic country data would be brought promptly to the attention of the Fund's Executive Board. If there continues to be no satisfactory explanation for the delay, the next monthly issue of *International Financial Statistics* could carry a footnote in the relevant data series indicating that publication of that monthly or quarterly series has been delayed. Such a delay would therefore likely carry a market penalty, since market participants may well reason that the delay reflected a desire to postpone the release of bad news. Wherever possible, countries should be encouraged to adopt a fixed time format for the publication of specific economic series. The Fund should also be vigilant to changes in coverage or definition of economic statistics if there is any presumption that such changes may reflect a desire to compromise the transparency of economic developments. In many cases, countries will see it in their own interest to improve the timeliness and transparency of their published economic statistics. To take but one relevant recent example, the Bank of Mexico began (in mid-April 1995) publishing daily data on money supply, intervention in foreign exchange markets, and current account developments.

A second constructive step would be the timely publication of IMF Article IV staff appraisals for individual countries. This might help market participants to gauge better the conduct of monetary, fiscal, and structural policies in these countries. Put in other words, it may help market participants to get a better fix on the fundamentals underlying

---

35. Article VIII, section 5, IMF Articles of Agreement.

36. Again, see Article VIII, section 5 of the Fund's articles.

exchange rates. In cases where those policy fundamentals are judged to be weak, one might also expect publication of these reports to add to market pressures for countries to take corrective action. Given the potential disciplinary clout of global capital markets, no country—even the very largest ones—can be indifferent to market evaluations of their policies as reflected, inter alia, in long-term bond yields and exchange market pressures. This is also the answer to long-standing concerns about lack of symmetry in Fund surveillance between industrial and developing countries. Peer pressure alone for better policies is not enough. Granted, the marketplace is already full of forecasts and policy analyses for these countries. But if, as Fischer (1994) suggests, the Fund has a particular expertise in the analysis of these macroeconomic policy fundamentals, then perhaps this analysis ought to be shared with those whose financial decisions affect interest rates and exchange rates.[37]

Some indication of the Fund's assessment of policy fundamentals—at least for the major industrial countries and some of the larger developing countries—already is published biannually in the Fund's *World Economic Outlook*. Also, the Fund annually publishes its assessment of capital-market developments in its *International Capital Markets Report*. And as was noted in chapter 1, it has since November 1994 been making public (for anyone requesting it) the part of its Article IV country reports that contain the factual information on recent economic developments. What it does not now publish is the part of Article IV country reports that gives the staff's *appraisal* of the country's economic policies and prospects.[38] But this is precisely the kind of analysis that should be useful to market participants in forging a view of fundamentals over the medium term. To get the ball rolling, countries should have permission to release these staff appraisals to the public.[39] Once a few G-7 countries set the right example, other countries would face calls to follow suit (lest they appear to be hiding a bad report card); put in other words, there would be a bit of "competitive transparency."

There are three principal objections to the publication of IMF staff appraisals. One is that by making these appraisals public, the confidential-

---

37. A related issue is whether published Fund assessments of country policies would be more or less frank than those of private market participants. On the one side, the Fund—unlike some private market analysts—need not worry that its country appraisals might compromise the marketing of country securities or the value of its own holdings of such securities. On the other side of the ledger, because the countries themselves are the Fund's clients, it is sometimes argued that published Fund criticism would need to be watered down (relative to that of private-market participants) so as not to unduly alienate its major shareholders.

38. These appraisals are much more comprehensive than those contained in the *World Economic Outlook*.

39. Because these documents are Fund documents, countries cannot release them of their own accord.

ity and frankness of IMF Article IV consultations would be undermined. Senior government officials might, for example, be deterred from discussing emerging weaknesses in the economy with the IMF mission for fear that these weaknesses would eventually be disclosed to the market. While such concerns merit serious consideration, their impact on the quality of consultation discussions can easily be exaggerated.

To begin with, Fund assessments of country policies (at least for G-7 countries and some larger developing countries) have been published for almost 15 years in the *World Economic Outlook* without apparently damaging the quality of consultations. To be sure, publication of staff appraisals would disclose more to the market and would provide a more comprehensive assessment of policies (and for more countries)—but the change would be a matter of degree, not of kind.

In addition, as is presently the case, there need be no requirement that each piece of information gathered in the consultation be included in the published report. Management and the Executive Board would have, as they do now, some discretion over what is included in published reports. The market does not need a tape recording of the entire Article IV consultation to form a view on fundamentals. What it could benefit from is a timely assessment of the country's economic policies and prospects from an independent official agency that specializes in the evaluation of macroeconomic and exchange rate policies. Nor is it clear that countries would have an incentive to talk less about problems under more liberal publication policies. In most cases, the mission will have some idea of the major problems facing the country prior to the consultation. Knowing that the Fund's assessment is going to be published could induce authorities to provide more information and analysis (than they do now) so as to increase the chances that the Fund assessment takes all the relevant information and arguments into account.

A second potential objection is that by publishing critical material in staff appraisals, the Fund will lay itself open to the (justifiable) charge of precipitating an exchange market crisis. This, too, is a concern that cannot be dismissed out of hand. Yet here also, I believe the objection is not convincing enough to carry the day.

It is not necessary—nor compatible with its purpose of giving "confidence to members"—for the Fund in these reports to flash in neon lights the message, "Currency X now overvalued, sell at once." As in reports issued by other official bodies (e.g., the US Federal Reserve on monetary policy), it is possible for market participants to "read between the lines." That has certainly been the practice with the reports that the Fund already publishes (e.g., the *World Economic Outlook*), and it would presumably continue to be the case for staff appraisals.

One also has to consider the counterfactual to giving the market more information. Once country policies get sufficiently off track, some market correction is almost inevitable. Better to catch it at an earlier stage when the correction is relatively small than to have the market at a later stage force a larger and less orderly adjustment. With the benefit of hindsight, wouldn't the market correction have been smaller and less costly if the market had pushed Mexico harder in, say, April/May 1994 rather than in December?

Market Discipline versus Official Financing

The less the weight placed on market discipline to induce corrective action, the greater the weight that will have to be placed on official resources to deal with private capital flows, debt servicing, and exchange market pressures and to encourage policy adjustments.[40] But that latter course of action is handicapped by another fact of life: since the private sector now has such a high stack of chips to play with, the official sector likewise needs to come up with a large stack to make a difference in the outcome (at least when defense of a fixed exchange rate, or a banking run, or a potential debt default, is involved). Yet under existing arrangements, marshaling official resources in these huge amounts is problematic (to say nothing of the moral hazard effects when they can be marshaled).

Nothing illustrates this last point better than the recent Mexican crisis. Once the crisis got under way, it soon became apparent that any international support package that could credibly alleviate the need for an involuntary rescheduling of Mexico's debt obligations would have to be sizable. In the end, the official sector was able to mobilize an extraordinary financial support package for Mexico. Examination of the two largest compo-

---

40. If there were an internationally agreed bankruptcy procedure for national governments, as suggested by Sachs (1994), this could perhaps reduce the need for official external finance. In Sachs's plan, the IMF might become the bankruptcy court, there would be a standstill on servicing old public and private debt, these debts could be later rescheduled or written down, and the debtor would be required to adopt corrective economic policies. He argues that under these conditions, the debtor would be able to maintain essential state services, the debtor's creditworthiness would be rebuilt, and (new) private international capital flows would meet the debtor's need for finance—without the costs and moral hazard associated with large official bailouts. But there is no such international bankruptcy code in place, and many tough questions and obstacles would have to be faced to secure its early enactment. For one thing, it would need to be decided how to supersede national bankruptcy laws. Alternatively, if the choice was to opt for more informal procedures that could facilitate a more orderly workout of potential defaults on sovereign bonds, it would need to be shown both how legal challenges to those procedures could be successfully withstood and how a diverse and numerous group of bond holders could be effectively organized. Moreover, questions about the likely effects of such a bankruptcy code would need to be addressed. For example, would spreads on sovereign bonds increase after its enactment, and if so, would debtors regard these increased borrowing costs (now) as worth the greater protection offered for a low probability event in the future? All of this does not mean that serious work into what would be involved in establishing such an international bankruptcy code is not worthwhile. Quite the contrary. But it does suggest that it probably wouldn't be wise to hold one's breath until the issue is resolved.

nents of that total, however, indicate why it is likely to be the exception that proves the rule.

The largest component is a $20 billion loan, funded from the US Treasury's Exchange Stabilization Fund. Recall that the Clinton administration was driven to this mode of financing only after it proved impossible to garner enough congressional support to obtain approval for an earlier $40 billion loan guarantee proposal. And this legislative opposition took hold despite the "special" stakes involved for the United States of *not* providing support for Mexico, including the potentially significant loss of US exports and jobs, the prospect of higher immigration, the negative feedback for any post-NAFTA trade liberalization proposals, the risk that a severe economic crisis by the emerging market economy most wedded to the "Washington policy consensus" could unravel support for it elsewhere,[41] and the damage to US leadership associated with failure to assist a next-door neighbor in its hour of need.

Moreover, even after Congress was let off the hook for funding the US contribution, congressional criticism of US assistance by no means ceased, including the charge that the package "bails out" wealthy Wall Street investors and weakens future incentives of creditors and borrowers to monitor risk (the moral hazard problem). After Mexico, what other emerging-market country could reasonably expect in a crisis to get US financial support on a scale anywhere near that of the Mexican deal?

The IMF component of the package, at over $17 billion, is likewise not easily replicable. Mexico's quota in the Fund is SDR1.75 billion (roughly, $2.5 billion). Mexico not only obtained the maximum cumulative access (300 percent of quota)—which is itself exceptional—but also received an additional $10 billion under the "exceptional circumstances" provision of current Fund access policy.[42] In addition, the funds were front-loaded more than is the normal case. This was the largest standby loan in IMF history. One has to ask how often—even in exceptional cases—the Fund's resources and its need to get the membership's full support will permit it to provide an industrial country or a relatively large emerging-market country with a loan equal to more than 700 percent of quota. Yet it is by no means uncommon nowadays for countries to record *monthly* reserve losses in excess of 100 percent of their Fund quotas.[43]

---

41. See Williamson and Haggard (1994) for a definition and analysis of the "Washington consensus" on policy reform.

42. Under current IMF access policy for standbys and extended arrangements, there are annual and cumulative access limits of 100 and 300 percent of quota, respectively—but no specific, quantitative limit in cases of "exceptional circumstances."

43. Admittedly, Mexico was such a large recipient of net private capital flows over 1990–94 that the need for an official rescue package of a size close to Mexico's may not arise for other emerging-market countries—even if they did suffer a large deterioration in market confidence. Still, securing support for official packages on the order of, say, $20 billion or so would be far from an easy undertaking.

Note should also be taken of the large changes in the composition of private capital flows to developing countries that have occurred over the past 15 years. In the buildup to the debt crisis, commercial bank loans represented over three-quarters of private capital flows to developing countries. That share fell to only 17 percent in the 1990–93 period. Now it is foreign direct investment (51 percent), portfolio equity flows (16 percent), and bonds (15 percent) that rule the roost (Fernandez-Arias and Montiel 1995). This carries a number of implications. Because holders of portfolio capital are well diversified, there is a strong presumption that a sharp decline in bond and equity prices in emerging markets would translate into only a modest decline in their wealth and thus pose less of a systemic threat in creditor countries than did the (temporary) bank insolvencies in the last debt crisis. At the same time, the more decentralized structure of bond and equity holdings implies that it will be more difficult (than during the peak influence of bank advisory committees) for the official sector to orchestrate a "workout" once a financial crisis occurs. The "catalytic" effect of an IMF program on other creditors is now also likely to be less direct than before. Increasingly, it is fund managers (and their shareholders) rather than commercial bankers that will pass judgment on the adequacy of an IMF program.

My point is not to suggest that the international support package for Mexico was unwarranted; all things considered, I believe that support was appropriate. Nor do I mean to imply that the evolution of private capital markets makes redundant the need for an international lender of last resort. It certainly does not. Instead, I simply want to emphasize that once the milk is on the floor for a large market borrower, it is now a much messier and more costly operation for the official sector to mop it up. There is therefore a much bigger premium than before in having a well-functioning "early warning system" in place.

The basic message for the Fund is also clear: when it comes to countries that have significant access to private capital markets, **the most potent channel for making Fund surveillance more effective is by affecting the market's evaluation of a country's policies**. Even if the Fund is able to convince the membership of an early need for a quota increase, the leverage on country policies coming from the Fund's own financial support will be less than it used to be (say, in the 1950s and 1960s) when private capital flows were much smaller. But this new "market-based" surveillance channel won't operate with much effect if the market doesn't know what the Fund's policy evaluation is. And the market can't know that (except in cases of countries with Fund programs) unless the Fund's policy evaluations are published on a timely basis.

The third objection to publication of Fund staff appraisals goes exactly in the opposite direction. It worries not that publication will have effects that are too large, but rather that it will have little or no market impact at all. This is a criticism that can only be evaluated with the test of time.

If Fund reports are judged by market participants to contain little useful information beyond what is already available from other sources in the private and public sectors, then clearly one will not have to worry about market reactions. On the other hand, if those reports demonstrate a capacity to convey an objective and well-grounded evaluation of country policies and prospects, I would expect their market impact to grow over time. One may not be able to tell much from the market reaction to the first few such reports, but after a year or two, it will be possible to tell whether publication had any influence on market views.

Suppose that given all these considerations, the Fund were to decide to go in the direction of sharing more of its appraisals of country policies with the markets. This still leaves a thorny practical problem to deal with—namely, how can the Fund provide a *timely* appraisal of its views to the markets? After all, a staff appraisal published six months ago may not convey information and guidance that is very useful for assessing today's situation, particularly if developments and risks have changed substantially over the intervening period.

I do not believe this is an unsurmountable problem for two reasons. First, in addition to publication of Article IV reports, the Fund has several other regular channels for disseminating its views to the markets. Since these do not all get published at the same time, this offers some flexibility in timing. Second, in those cases where the Fund judges that it would be helpful to share its views with the market right away, a short press statement may serve the purpose. Indeed, in mid-April, the Fund did just that, when it released a press statement by the managing director on the Bank of Japan's decision to cut its discount rate. That statement is reproduced on page 42. Note that in addition to expressing IMF support for the Japanese discount rate cut, the statement also offers the Fund's view on recent exchange rate developments for the G-3 countries, on the need for an early interest rate increase in the United States, and on medium-term policy requirements in the United States, Europe, and Japan.

Peer Pressure and the Interim Committee

On the peer pressure front, it is time to get the Interim Committee more involved. This is the only forum where finance ministers representing virtually the entire global community meet twice a year. Yet to this point, the committee seems to have no continuing mandate. It has real business to do when there are initiatives that need high-level approval—for example, approving the creation of a Systemic Transformation Facility for the transition economies, or giving the okay to an increase in Fund access limits, or trying to cut a deal on SDR allocation. But on the more frequent occasions when no such initiatives are in play, much of the committee's time is spent in a round of ministerial interventions on the world economic

NEWS BRIEF

FOR IMMEDIATE RELEASE

Number 95/12 April 14, 1995

Camdessus Welcomes Bank of Japan's Decision to Cut Discount Rate

Michel Camdessus, Managing Director of the International Monetary Fund, today made the following statement:

"I welcome today's 75-basis-point cut in the official discount rate by the Bank of Japan. Coming on the heels of the interest rate reduction by the German Bundesbank at the end of March, this action should also help to alleviate pressures on foreign exchange markets," Camdessus said.

"The large and rapid exchange rate changes that we have seen recently pose a risk of higher inflation in the United States, threaten to weaken the expansion in Europe, and could jeopardize recovery in Japan. I believe these monetary policy actions were appropriate to counter these threats," he added.

"I believe it is now opportune for the United States to complement these actions by raising its short-term interest rates. This would contribute to a strengthening of the dollar, which would be appropriate given its role as the key international currency. It would also help contain the domestic inflationary pressures that will result from a weak dollar.

"Recent exchange rate movements have also accentuated the need for broader policy actions in a medium-term perspective. Since the early 1980s, a persistent current account deficit has increased U.S. net foreign liabilities, and contributed to the decline of the dollar. A significant and sustained reduction in the U.S. external deficit requires a corresponding rise in the relatively low level of U.S. national saving. The most effective way to increase U.S. saving is through more ambitious fiscal consolidation. Early and credible steps to reduce further the U.S. federal deficit would send an appropriate signal to the markets that the problem was being addressed, provide the additional saving required for an improvement in the external balance, and make the dollar less vulnerable to shifting market sentiments. In Europe also, intensification of efforts at fiscal consolidation during this period of recovery should have higher priority. For Japan, stronger efforts at deregulation and market opening measures will contribute to the efficient operation of the domestic economy and may help to reduce the pressure on the yen. Therefore, it would be helpful from both a short-term as well as a medium-term perspective for Japan to accelerate this process on a priority basis, including the announced measures," Camdessus said.

outlook and related subjects, with very little spontaneity, interchange, or effect.

Why not better use the opportunity to have ministers respond to the specific policy diagnoses and recommendations made for their economies by their peers? At the end of every IMF Executive Board meeting on an Article IV country consultation, the chairman offers a summing up of the discussion—aimed at appraising the economy's recent performance and at identifying what policy measures would improve it. But if such international surveillance is to be effective, it is essential that some effort be made to determine whether a country has in fact followed up on those policy recommendations, and if not, why.

The Interim Committee is an attractive forum for conducting such a follow-up. Representation is at a very senior level, and membership is near universal. To keep the process manageable, it might begin with the 10 or 15 largest member countries, perhaps handling five or six country cases at each meeting; this would leave enough time for a genuine interchange of views on the subject country's situation. The idea of a follow-up mechanism was first aired in a 1985 Group of Ten report. The Fund's board adopted in August 1992 a low-key version of it that could involve a confidential exchange of letters between the managing director and the finance minister. But it seems preferable to do the follow-up in a multilateral rather than bilateral setting and thus to mobilize somewhat more forcefully—when called for—the finger of public shame. It might even be considered whether it would be worthwhile to publish a summation of the Interim Committee's discussion of country cases, thereby adding an additional channel for sharing official views on policies with the market.

More Awareness of the Views of the Non–G-7

A related question that touches on both exchange rate policy and the underlying policy fundamentals is how the views of non–G-7 countries can be brought to bear on the decisions of the G-7. As noted earlier, suggestions have ranged from creation of a (higher level) Fund Council, to establishment of a subcommittee of the Fund's Executive Board to deal with international monetary issues, to designation of the G-7 as an official committee of the Fund.

Adopting the principle of Occam's razor, a simpler and preferable proposal would be to have the host of the next G-7 ministerial (or deputies) meeting get together with the Fund's Executive Board a few days ahead of the meeting to inform them of the agenda and to hear their concerns and suggestions. He or she could then return a few days after the meeting to give a summary of the G-7 discussion and to answer questions.[44] In

---

44. As noted earlier, another option would be for the G-7 to ask the managing director of the Fund to undertake this task.

that way, the rest of the non–G-7 countries could legitimately feel that their voice had been heard on matters that affect them, and they would know something of what happened in G-7 meetings beyond what they read in the newspaper. For its part, the G-7 could keep its smallness and informality and have at least some assurance of confidentiality.

Over the longer term, it is likely that the G-7 of its own accord will want to invite some of the larger developing countries to join the group because of their weight in the world economy. Even in that case, G-7 reporting to those outside the tent would still make sense.

Reexamining the Concepts of Exchange Rate Manipulation and Unfair Competitive Advantage

Turning to the last item on the modest agenda: the IMF and its members need to reexamine the concepts of "exchange rate manipulation" and "unfair competitive advantage." Specifically, are they are operationally useful in a world in which almost all countries intervene in exchange markets to some extent or another and in which countries follow very different paces and practices on capital market liberalization?[45] These concepts were included in the Fund's Articles of Agreement to ensure that antisocial or beggar-thy-neighbor policies would be identified and discouraged—whatever a country's exchange arrangements. While the Fund's articles clearly stipulate that it is the obligation of all members to avoid such practices, the reality is that at present there is little consensus on what guidelines are to be employed to identify their presence and on whether the object of concern should be exchange rates per se or underlying monetary or capital-market policies. Reflecting this ambiguity, practically no countries have been charged in the Fund over the past 20 years with violating their international exchange rate obligations.

Continuing with the present approach is neither desirable nor sustainable. It is not desirable because there are indications that countries are concerned about other countries' exchange rate policies and may resort to national protectionist (trade) measures if these concerns are not addressed in an agreed, multilateral forum. It is not sustainable because structural changes in the world economy are apt to make the perception of "fairness" in exchange rate policy increasingly important.

In the United States, the 1988 Omnibus Trade and Competitiveness Act requires the secretary of the Treasury to consider whether countries "manipulate the rate of exchange between their currencies and the U.S. dollar for the purpose of preventing effective balance of payments adjustment or gaining competitive advantage in international trade." As such,

---

45. IMF Article IV states that "each member shall . . . avoid manipulating exchange rates or the international monetary system in order to prevent effective balance of payments adjustment or to gain an unfair competitive advantage over other members. . . . "

the US Treasury has since reported semiannually to the Congress on alleged "manipulating countries." In these reports, manipulation is typically taken to arise when the country employs foreign exchange and/or capital controls to reduce upward pressure on its currency—what one might call "competitive nonappreciation." Suffice to say that in past years, several Asian developing countries were judged by the Treasury to be guilty of manipulation.

While other countries do not have similar domestic requirements to report on "manipulators," complaints about exchange rate "dumping" have surfaced on several occasions. For example, some regarded the fall of the pound and the lira (to say nothing of the even larger decline in the Swedish krona) that was associated with the marked easing of monetary policy after the currencies' 1992 departure from the ERM as having conferred an unfair competitive advantage on the United Kingdom and Italy (relative to their partners who stayed in the ERM). Even the abrupt fall of the Russian ruble in late 1994 was seen by some observers as raising the specter that countries could manage bad news so as to induce a large depreciation in the market and thereby reap an unfair competitive advantage. In defense, many countries could argue that almost all countries intervene on occasion in exchange markets to check what they regard as market excesses, that temporary imposition of—or temporary increases in—restrictions on capital inflows is a legitimate way to deal with surges in volatile capital inflows, and that monetary policy easing in the face of domestic recession is entirely appropriate even if it induces a large depreciation of the (floating) domestic currency.

Given these difficulties of interpretation, couldn't we just let sleeping dogs lie? Probably not, and for at least four reasons. First, the prospective further dismantling of trade barriers—both global (through the Uruguay Round) and regional (through the North American Free Trade Area, Asia Pacific Economic Cooperation, and the Free Trade Area of the Americas)—will remove much of what is left of the protective cushion and will increase competitive pressures. This in turn should make countries more sensitive to exchange rate–induced changes in competitive advantage—especially if this competitive advantage is perceived as "unfairly" gained.

Second, as the weight of developing countries in the world economy increases further, and as these countries become more important trading partners of the industrial countries, the focus of attention is likely to shift away from G-7 exchange rate relationships to those between industrial and developing countries (and not only in the Pacific).[46] Again, complaints about manipulation will be harder to ignore, much as were earlier complaints about unfair foreign trade practices.

---

46. Some of these issues already attracted considerable attention in the mid-to-late 1980s with respect to the exchange rate policies of several newly industrialized countries; see Balassa and Williamson (1987).

Third, to the extent that developing countries continue to confront large swings in private capital flows, they are likely to engage heavily (as they have over the past three years) in intervention and sterilization operations so as to smooth the impact of these flows on their export competitiveness and on their monetary aggregates. But such smoothing operations could raise questions about manipulation.

And fourth, several developing countries already have very large stocks of international reserves. Management of those reserve positions—particularly if not carried out in a cooperative manner with the reserve-currency countries—could have nontrivial effects in exchange markets.

I do not want to prejudge whether it will prove feasible to come up with a workable definition of exchange rate manipulation in a world of widespread exchange-market intervention and changing policies and practices toward international capital flows. It may turn out that the issue cannot be resolved by specifying a small set of principles or indicators. Perhaps what constitutes manipulation can only emerge as case law, after a series of real-life country situations are examined.

But I am convinced that the international community should try to resolve the issue one way or another so that the concept of antisocial exchange rate (or capital market policy) behavior carries some agreed, operational international content. The IMF is precisely the forum in which such issues should be discussed on a multilateral basis—much in the same way that countries have by now become accustomed to bringing their trade complaints to the GATT (and now the WTO). Otherwise, countries will make their own interpretations of manipulation and unfair competitive advantage, with adverse consequences for world trade and investment. It is time for the Fund and its members to get on with that job.

Concluding Observations

Looking down the road, two messages about the future of the exchange rate system are worth highlighting.

One is that the menu for international monetary reform should contain more than two entries. There *is* a viable alternative to both fundamental reform of the current system and to standing pat with existing arrangements. When G-7 leaders meet in Halifax in mid-June, they ought to give serious consideration to modest changes in existing arrangements, with the aim of rendering G-3 exchange rate policy more credible and consistent, of making private capital markets smarter, and of improving the system's early warning capabilities (for industrial and developing countries alike). Such a modest agenda also offers a practical way to underpin the systemic role of the IMF—not for its own sake but in the broader interest of reducing the frequency, size, and duration of exchange rate misalignments and of associated financial market strains.

The second message is that if tangible progress is to be made in improving the functioning of the exchange rate system and of private capital markets it will need to be built on specific, concrete recommendations. Expressing a desire for greater exchange rate stability or expressing support for a strengthening of Fund surveillance will not by themselves get us very far. The key questions today are specific "how" questions.

How, as Volcker and Gyohten (1992) put it, can a framework be devised in which authorities can develop "some reasoned and broad judgments about what range of exchange rate fluctuations [among the key currencies] is reasonable and tolerable, and what is not?" How can the key-currency countries reconcile their domestic requirements for monetary policy with an enhanced effort to identify and to correct large misalignments at an earlier stage? How can international peer pressure best supplement national efforts to rein in errant fiscal policies? How can the IMF improve its early warning performance in both industrial and developing countries? And how can the disciplinary role of private capital markets be strengthened and made more consistent and less abrupt, so that the need for large, official support packages is reduced?

For starters, you have my set of answers.

Annex: Short-Run Exchange Rate Variability and Economic Performance

A recurring criticism of existing exchange rate arrangements is that high short-run variability of nominal and real exchange rates seriously handicaps economic performance.[1] This annex explores the link between short-term exchange rate variability and economic performance. After reviewing the basic facts about short-term exchange rate variability, I take up in turn effects on international trade, investment, and economic growth.

Facts about Short-Run Variability

If there was a contest to describe short-run exchange rate variability under managed floating in 25 words or less, my entry would be: much higher than before (under Bretton Woods), no tendency to change over time, and like that for other asset prices.

Figures 1a through 1c show that for the three key-currency countries, short-run (monthly), nominal exchange rate variability has been much higher—on the order of three to five times as high—under managed floating than it was under the last decade of the Bretton Woods period. The qualitative nature of this conclusion is not altered if one replaces nominal exchange rates with real ones, or switches from bilateral to effective exchange rates, or does the comparison with an earlier part of the Bretton Woods period, or employs either higher frequency data (daily) or other measures of short-run variability.

Table 1 illustrates that if the period of managed floating is broken down into four subperiods, there is no discernible tendency for the variability

---

1. See, for example, Bretton Woods Commission (1994a) and Ohno (1994).

Figure 1a Volatility of nominal exchange rates, Japanese yen/US dollar, 1961–95

percent change from previous month

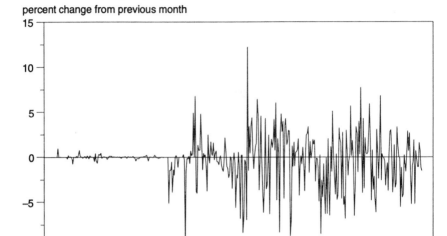

Sources: Mussa et al. 1994a; IMF, *International Financial Statistics.*

of bilateral dollar exchange rates to decline over time.[2] Variability for the pound sterling, the French franc, and the deutsche mark is actually higher in the second half of the floating rate period than in the first half, and short-run variability for the Canadian dollar and the yen is only slightly lower.

Table 2 documents that short-run variability of nominal exchange rates (under managed floating) has exceeded by a wide margin the variability of consumer price indices but has been comparable to that of other asset prices: equity prices and prices of agricultural raw materials, minerals and metals, and food show similar variability, while petroleum and gold prices show much higher variability.

But what about the possibility that the observed high degree of short-term exchange rate variability under managed floating is just a coincidence rather than a characteristic of the exchange rate regime? Based on the available empirical evidence, this possibility must be judged most unlikely.

Because real exchange rates can be defined under any type of exchange arrangements, and because it is real—not nominal—exchange rates that

---

2. If one moves from monthly or quarterly exchange rate variability to variability over much longer periods, then the results may be quite different (see Sapir et al. 1994), but that takes us away from short-term exchange rate variability and closer to misalignment issues.

Figure 1b Volatility of nominal exchange rates, deutsche mark/US dollar, 1961–95

percent change from previous month

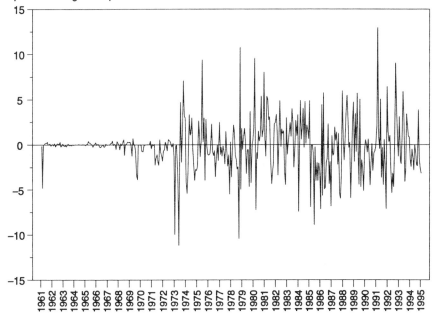

Sources: Mussa et al. 1994a; IMF, *International Financial Statistics.*

matter for resource allocation decisions, it is natural to consider how real exchange rates have behaved under alternative exchange rate regimes. In that connection, two pieces of evidence are relevant. First, most of the short-run variability in real exchange rates under managed floating reflects the variability of nominal exchange rates—not of relative inflation rates.[3] Second, empirical studies (Mussa (1986, 1990) that have examined real exchange rate variability across a wide variety of experience (using both time-series and cross-section data) have found strong evidence that short-run variability of real exchange rates is systematically higher under floating rate regimes than under fixed rate regimes.[4] Consistent with this proposition, one can discern a trend decrease in short-term variability of nominal and real exchange rates for a number of European currencies (e.g., the Belgian franc, the Dutch guilder, the French franc, the Austrian schilling, the Danish krone) over 1973–92 (see table 3) that tracks roughly the increasing tightness of their nominal link to the deutsche mark over this period (Mussa and Isard 1993).

---

3. See Mussa et al. (1994a) and table 2. The correlation between nominal and real exchange rates becomes stronger as one moves from high- to lower-frequency data; see Obstfeld (1995).

4. Most researchers attribute this result to the greater "stickiness" of goods prices relative to asset prices.

**Figure 1c Volatility of nominal exchange rates, deutsche mark/
Japanese yen, 1961–95**

percent change from previous month

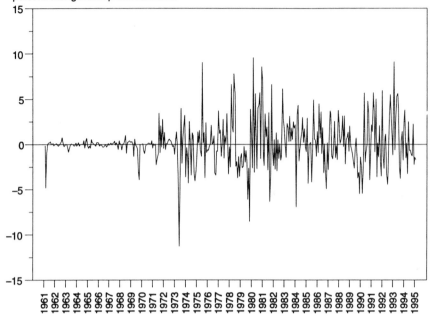

Sources: Mussa et al. 1994a; IMF, *International Financial Statistics*.

Thus far, the discussion has been solely about exchange rate variability. But concerns typically deal with exchange rate *uncertainty*. Is it reasonable to regard the former as a good proxy for the latter? Judging from the experience of the past 20 years, the answer is yes. By now, it is well established that most short-run exchange rate variability under managed floating has been *un*anticipated (Mussa 1990; Frankel and Rose 1995). No matter whether forecasts of the future spot exchange rate are obtained from the forward exchange rate, or from survey data on exchange rate expectations, or from time-series processes, or from rational expectations models, it turns out that only a small proportion of changes in exchange rates are anticipated by investors. Indeed, empirical tests of bias in the forward market usually show a pattern whereby the exchange rate not only fails (on average) to move in line with the predictions of the interest differential or the forward discount, but in fact moves in the opposite direction.[5]

In sum, little violence is done to reality by equating a floating rate regime with relatively large uncertainty about the short-term course of

---

5. See Lewis (1995) and Frankel and Rose (1995). The fact that several high interest rate currencies in the ERM experienced depreciations in 1992–93 probably has improved the track record of market indicators in forecasting the direction of exchange rate changes.

Table 1 Short-term variability of exchange rates among major currencies, 1973–94 (standard deviations of monthly percentage changes)

Bilateral exchange rates versus US dollar	April 1973– March 1979	April 1979– September 1983	October 1983– March 1988	April 1988– December 1994
Nominal				
Canadian dollar	1.3	1.4	1.2	1.3
Deutsche mark	3.4	3.2	3.6	3.5
French franc	3.1	3.3	3.4	3.4
Japanese yen	2.9	3.6	3.1	3.0
Pound sterling	2.6	3.2	3.6	3.8
Real, based on consumer prices				
Canadian dollar	1.4	1.5	1.2	1.3
Deutsche mark	3.5	3.2	3.6	3.5
French franc	3.2	3.3	3.4	3.5
Japanese yen	3.0	3.7	3.2	2.9
Pound sterling	2.7	3.5	3.7	3.8

Sources: Mussa and Isard (1993); IMF, *International Financial Statistics.*

both nominal and real exchange rates. The issue hinges then on whether this higher level of uncertainty has serious adverse feedback effects on economic performance.

Exchange Rate Uncertainty and Foreign Trade

Initially, concerns about the effects of high, short-term volatility of exchange rates centered on the volume of international trade. As shown in table 4, the volume of international trade continued to grow faster than that of real output during the floating rate period. But until recently, the margin by which trade growth has exceeded real output growth, as well as the average rate of growth of world trade itself, has declined with the transition from the Bretton Woods regime to the regime of managed floating. On average, the volume of world trade grew 3 percent faster than world real output in the 1960s, 1.6 percent faster in the 1970s, and only 1 percent faster in the 1980s. From 1991 to 1994, however, world trade growth rebounded to again exceed output growth by almost 3 percent.

If exchange rate uncertainty has increased under managed floating while the growth of trade has simultaneously slowed, couldn't the former be accounting for the latter? After all, wouldn't an increase in risk lead

Table 2 Relative volatility of nominal exchange rates, 1973–94

Exchange rates and price indices	Standard deviation of monthly percentage change		Average absolute monthly percentage change	
	1973–80	1981–94	1973–80	1981–94
Nominal exchange rates				
Deutsche mark/US dollar	3.45	3.48	2.47	2.72
Yen/US dollar	3.09	3.21	2.07	2.51
Deustche mark/yen	3.43	2.82	2.55	2.23
Consumer price indices				
United States	0.33	0.26	0.75	0.39
Germany	0.30	0.26	0.41	0.27
Japan	0.96	0.50	0.93	0.41
Equity price indices				
United States[a]	4.00	3.44	3.05	2.55
Germany[b]	..	4.88	..	3.73
Japan	3.18	4.43	2.40	3.34
Commodity price indices				
Agricultural raw materials	4.02	2.61	3.17	1.84
Minerals and metals	4.12	3.48	3.07	2.50
Food	5.03	2.85	3.96	2.16
Petroleum	30.64	9.20	5.67	5.54
Gold	8.68	4.24	6.08	2.99

.. = data not available

a. US equity index is Dow Jones.
b. German equity price indices begin in 1983.

Series begin in March 1973.

Sources: Goldstein and Isard (1992); IMF, *International Financial Statistics*; Data Resources, Inc. (for equity price indices).

risk-averse individuals to reduce their efforts in the risky activity (exports) in favor of concentrating on less risky endeavors (production for the domestic market)?

It turns out that theory is not quite so cooperative. To get the conclusion that an increase in exchange rate uncertainty will always produce a fall in the supply of exports, one needs to assume that individuals display a particular behavior toward risk. The ambiguity arises because an increase in risk carries both a substitution effect and an income effect. The switch toward less risky activities, described above, comes from the substitution effect. The income effect carries the opposite sign: when risk increases,

Table 3   Short-term variability of exchange rates among European currencies, 1973–92 (standard deviations of monthly percentage changes)

Bilateral exchange rates versus deutsche mark	April 1973– March 1979	April 1979– September 1983	October 1983– March 1988	April 1988– December 1992
Nominal				
Belgian franc	0.9	1.2	0.4	0.4
Netherlands guilder	1.2	0.7	0.4	0.5
Danish krone	1.3	1.0	0.6	0.6
Austrian schilling	0.8	0.3	0.3	0.4
French franc	2.1	1.4	0.9	0.5
Italian lira	3.3	1.2	0.9	2.1
Irish pound	3.0	1.0	1.2	0.4
Swiss franc	2.3	1.7	1.2	1.4
Pound sterling	3.0	3.4	2.5	2.3
Swedish krone	1.8	3.1	1.3	2.2
Norwegian krone	1.7	1.8	1.6	1.2
Finnish markka	2.2	2.2	1.1	2.8
Spanish peseta	4.2	2.5	1.3	1.7
Portuguese escudo	3.0	3.1	1.0	1.1
Real, based on consumer prices				
Belgian franc	1.1	1.3	0.4	0.5
Netherlands guilder	1.4	0.8	0.6	0.7
Danish krone	1.5	1.1	0.9	0.7
Austrian schilling	0.8	0.5	0.5	0.6
French franc	2.1	1.5	0.9	0.6
Italian lira	3.3	1.2	1.0	2.2
Irish pound	3.4	2.2	1.5	0.6
Swiss franc	2.4	1.7	1.2	1.4
Pound sterling	3.0	3.5	2.6	2.4
Swedish krone	1.9	3.2	1.5	2.4
Norwegian krone	1.7	2.0	1.7	1.3
Finnish markka	2.2	2.3	1.2	2.9
Spanish peseta	4.0	2.6	1.4	1.7
Portuguese escudo	3.4	3.2	1.4	1.3

Source: Mussa and Isard (1993).

Table 4 Growth of world trade volume and output, 1870–1994
(average annual growth rate, percentage)

	1870–1913	1950–60	1960–70	1970–80	1980–90	1991–94
World trade	3.9	6.5	8.3	5.2	4.3	5.3
World GDP	2.5	4.2	5.3	3.6	3.3	2.4
Difference	1.4	2.3	3.0	1.6	1.0	2.9

Sources: UNCTAD, 1994; IMF, *World Economic Outlook*, various issues.

expected utility of export revenue declines, and this can be offset by exporting more. As demonstrated by De Grauwe (1988) and others, only if the substitution effect dominates the income effect does an increase in exchange rate uncertainty lead to a lower supply of exports. Some early studies that produced more definitive predictions did so only by employing a more restrictive form of the utility function (constant absolute risk aversion) that by assumption eliminates the income effect.

If the predictions of theory are not definitive (even about the sign of the trade volume/exchange rate variability nexus), what about the empirical evidence? Fortunately, the effect of exchange rate uncertainty on the volume of trade is by now one of the most well-trodden areas of quantitative international economics, encompassing well over a hundred empirical studies. These studies are of two types: time-series studies of a country's total trade flows and cross-section studies of bilateral trade patterns.

In the time-series studies, the typical practice is to regress a country's volume of total exports (or total imports) on the level of real income or real output in the importing countries (country), on relative traded goods' prices, and on a measure of (real or nominal) short-run exchange rate variability. In my view, these time-series studies offer powerful evidence because the experimental conditions are abnormally propitious. The main independent variable of interest—namely, short-run exchange rate variability—has undergone a huge change in behavior as between the fixed and floating rate periods (see figure 1a–c); there is no problem, therefore, with finding enough variation over time in exchange rate variability to make a difference.

Just as crucial, there is a well-established model—the imperfect substitutes trade model—that allows one to hold constant the other determinants of trade.[6] This is crucial because some of these other determinants also changed markedly with the transition to managed floating. For example, as noted earlier, real output growth was on average much lower during the floating period than in the two decades preceding it, and real

---

6. For an exposition of this trade model, as well as a review of the empirical evidence using it, see Hooper and Marquez (1993) and Goldstein and Khan (1985).

output growth has long been shown to be the single most important factor influencing aggregate trade flows.

Likewise, trade barriers have fallen sharply over time. In this latter connection, the margin by which world trade growth exceeded world output growth was only 2.3 percent in the 1950s despite the maintenance of fixed exchange rates, but this presumably reflected in part the lesser stimulus to trade afforded by trade liberalization measures during that period and the return of European nations to current account convertibility only in 1958.

The cross-sectional studies seek to take advantage of the very large data base on bilateral trade flows and of the considerable variation in the degree of exchange rate variability across countries. This normally provides samples far larger than can be obtained in time-series studies of total trade flows. The rub is that the modeling of bilateral trade flows is more difficult than that for total trade flows. Noneconomic factors (like use of a common language or political ties) have to be confronted in modeling bilateral trade, whereas these factors can be ignored when modeling total trade flows.[7] In addition, simultaneous-equations bias is more of a potential problem since countries may act to limit exchange rate variability with their more important bilateral trading partners.

In the early cross-sectional studies, authors employed a variant of the imperfect substitutes trade model (real income and measures of bilateral price competitiveness) to hold other things equal. In the more recent studies, resort has been made to the "gravity" model for this purpose. The gravity model hypothesizes that trade between two countries is proportional to the product of their sizes (measured, say, by the product of their GNPs) and inversely related to the distance between them. Distance is a proxy not only for transport costs but also for familiarity. The level of real per capita income is sometimes added to capture the notion that as countries get richer, they tend to specialize and trade more.

An economical way to summarize the evidence from time-series studies is to note the conclusions of four comprehensive surveys of empirical work carried over the past 10 years.[8] An IMF study (1984a, 36) concluded that

The large majority of empirical studies on the impact of exchange rate variability on the volume of international trade are unable to establish a systematically significant link between exchange rate variability on the volume of international trade, whether on an aggregated or bilateral basis.

---

7. Some might argue that this is less of a problem because these noneconomic factors are typically time-invariant and thus can be easily distinguished in panel data sets from exchange rate dispersion that does vary over time.

8. I suppose a skeptic might still argue that the conclusions of these surveys are suspect because earlier research did not pay adequate attention to questions of stationarity and other concerns of more recent time-series inference.

Edison and Melvin (1990, 28), reviewing the empirical evidence six years later, reached a similar verdict:

> One certainly cannot examine the empirical evidence reviewed in this section, or the earlier papers not examined here, and claim that greater exchange rate variability reduces the volume of international trade.

Even the Commission of the European Communities' 1990 report, *One Market, One Money*, which is so supportive of the advantages of a single currency, acknowledges (73) that "the empirical research has not found any robust relationship between exchange rate variability and trade."

Most recently, Sapir et al. (1994, 13) characterize the existing empirical studies, as well as their own estimates, as follows:

> To sum up, no clear evidence of a significant adverse effect of volatility on trade has emerged from our analysis, except during the interwar period. This conclusion is actually representative of the whole literature concerning the postwar period.

A negative effect of exchange rate variability on trade volumes is less of an oddity in the cross-sectional studies than in the time-series ones, but again, no systematic link emerges. Just as relevant, in those (relatively few) studies where exchange rate variability is found to have a significant negative effect, the *size* of that effect is small and, where comparisons across time periods are available, *declining over time*.

The most comprehensive and careful of the studies of bilateral trade patterns is that of Frankel and Wei (1995). They employ a gravity model of bilateral trade flows and take account of the potential simultaneity between bilateral flows and bilateral exchange rate variability. They estimate that completely eliminating nominal exchange rate volatility worldwide (that is, putting the whole world on immutably fixed exchange rates) would have increased the volume of world trade in 1980 by less than one-hundredth of 1 percent![9] In another calculation, they estimate that eliminating altogether exchange rate variability in the European Community would have increased the volume of intra-EC trade by even less.[10] Gagnon (1993), employing a simulation model, also finds small effects. Specifically, he estimates that a switch from the Bretton Woods regime

---

9. If no account is taken of simultaneity between bilateral exchange rate variability and bilateral trade flows, the effect of exchange rate uncertainty emerges as much larger. In that case, elimination of exchange rate uncertainty worldwide would increase the volume of world trade by 22 percent.

10. The effects of eliminating exchange rate variability in the European Community are smaller because, inter alia, the degree of exchange rate variability is much lower to begin with than it is worldwide and because exchange rate variability would still exist with respect to its external trade with non-EC countries. If no account is taken of simultaneity, Frankel and Wei (1995) estimate that elimination of European exchange rate variability would increase intra-European trade by an estimated 14 percent.

Table 5   Currency derivatives: annual turnover, 1986–93
(millions of contracts traded, except where noted)

Type of contract	1986	1987	1988	1989	1990	1991	1992	1993
Currency futures	19.7	20.8	22.1	27.5	29.1	29.2	30.7	38.0
Currency options	13.0	18.3	18.2	20.7	18.9	22.9	23.4	23.8
Total	32.7	39.1	40.3	48.2	48.0	52.1	54.1	61.8
Notional principal value (billions of US dollars)								
Currency swaps	..	365.6	639.1	898.2	1,155.1	1,614.3	1,720.8	..

.. = data not available.

Source: Goldstein et al. (1994).

to the floating exchange rate regime of the 1970s would have reduced global international trade by roughly 1 percent.

Frankel and Wei (1995) report a consistent tendency for the estimates of exchange rate variability on trade to decline as they move from the 1960s to the 1990s. (Indeed, by 1990, the coefficient on short-run exchange rate variability actually takes on a positive sign and is statistically significant, both for nominal and real exchange rate variability.)

What could be behind this apparent secular decline in the effect of exchange rate variability on trade flows? The most plausible explanation is the greater availability of instruments for hedging against exchange rate risk. As indicated in the upper panel of table 5, the number of currency futures and options contracts traded on organized exchanges worldwide expanded from 33 million in 1986 to 62 million contracts in 1993. Activity in the over-the-counter markets apparently increased even faster; as seen in the lower panel of table 5, the notional principal value of currency swaps rose from $366 billion in 1987 to $1.721 trillion in 1992.

Admittedly, as noted by the Bretton Woods Commission (1994a), hedging involves costs, not all risks can be hedged, and not all hedges are perfect. Also, as argued by Kenen (1994c), firms may not know enough about the longer-term pattern of their payments and receipts (under floating rates) to make informed hedging choices. Moreover, derivatives can be employed for speculative position taking as well as for hedging purposes, and high exchange rate variability might be taken to increase the incentives to undertake both types of activities.

Nevertheless, it seems difficult to argue that this explosion in the market for currency-related derivative instruments did not make it easier and less expensive to hedge against exchange rate uncertainty. Since OTC hedging instruments (unlike their exchange traded counterparts) can be custom-tailored to meet a firm's particular hedging needs and since currency swaps are now routinely available for maturities extending up to 7 to 10 years, their rapid rate of growth weakens the argument that available hedging instruments still do not meet the needs of many market participants.

It is also relevant to note the findings of Eichengreen and Irwin (1995), who used a gravity model to study the effect of exchange rate volatility on trade during the interwar period (when trade volume fell by 30 percent between 1929 and 1932 and was still 10 percent below 1929 levels in 1938). They attribute the large negative effects of volatility on trade during this period in part to the absence of well-developed and economical hedging instruments and to the lack of experience with floating rates.

A second factor that too may have contributed to a secularly declining impact of exchange variability on trade volumes is the expansion of multinational firms. As argued by Dobson (1994b), large multinationals are apt to be better placed than others (particularly, small and medium-sized domestic firms) to shield themselves from exchange rate variability by locating production on both sides of major exchange rate relationships and by using internal matching to reduce the need for hedging.[11] In a related vein, Goldsborough (1981) has posited that intrafirm trade is likely to be less price-responsive than conventional trade because goods produced by multinationals are often tailored to the firm's particular manufacturing and distribution needs and thus have fewer close substitutes than the more standardized alternatives produced on the open market. In addition, independent producers can respond quicker to relative price changes because they need not be concerned with the effects of their actions on affiliates in other countries. Goldsborough (1981) finds that estimated price elasticities are lower for intrafirm trade than for conventional trade. Unfortunately, I know of no later empirical studies that attempt to replicate Goldsborough's findings on more recent data samples. Caves (1982) reports that various studies have found that multinationals have been active in anticipating exchange rate changes during a series of exchange rate crises but does not indicate whether multinationals were more successful in that endeavor than conventional firms.

If these arguments about the hedging advantages and lower price sensitivity of multinational firms were valid, then a secular increase in the weight of such corporations in both the world economy and in the conduct of international trade would be expected, *ceteris paribus*, to reduce over time the impact of a given degree of exchange rate variability on trade.

According to United Nations data, there are now about 37,000 multinational firms (although some double counting may be present). These firms control some 200,000 foreign affiliates, which employ some 73 million people and have sales of nearly $5 trillion—more than the value ($4.7 billion) of global exports and factor services (UNCTAD 1994).

Table 6, adopted from Graham (1995), indicates that foreign direct investment (largely representing equity and debt held by business firms

---

11. It is also likely the case that workers find it more difficult to hedge against exchange rate uncertainty than do investors.

Table 6 Annual compound growth rates of worldwide income, international trade, and foreign direct investment, 1981–90

	Percent[a]
Foreign direct investment outflows	24
Foreign direct investment stocks	16
Sales of multinational corporations	15
Exports of goods and nonfactor services	12
World gross domestic product	9

a. Derived from nominal values expressed in US dollars.

Source: Graham (1995).

in affiliated corporations located in nations other than the home nation of the investor firm) grew rapidly during the 1980s—considerably faster than either world trade or world income. Bergsten and Graham note also that growth rates of FDI probably understate the true extent of the "internationalization" of business over the past decade since these figures exclude the spread of nontraditional forms of international business, such as strategic alliances. They report, in addition, that international trade itself is becoming increasingly dominated by the operations of multinational corporations. For example, in 1989 about 21 percent of total US exports of goods and services were accounted for by exports shipped by US parent firms to their overseas affiliates, and another 18 percent represented exports of foreign-owned enterprises in the United States to their home countries. By UN estimates (UNCTAD 1994), about a third of world trade is now accounted for by intrafirm trade.

Data on trends in intrafirm trade for industrial countries are hard to come by. Grant et al. (1993), however, have been able to piece together (from various sources) some estimates of intrafirm trade as a percentage of trade by national multinational corporation parents (that is, exports by MNC parents to affiliates abroad as a percentage of exports from MNC parents resident in the country noted). In brief, they find that the share of intrafirm trade has been increasing over time in all three of the industrial countries (the United States, West Germany, and Belgium) in their sample. In the United States, for example, the share of intrafirm trade increased from 28 percent of MNC parents exports in 1982 to 37 percent in 1989; in Belgium and West Germany, the data refer to the 1960s and 1970s, and generally show larger percentage increases. Again, these developments in the globalization of business seem consistent with a secularly declining effect of exchange rate variability on trade volumes.

To this point, the discussion has dealt only with effects on trade volumes (as producers shift from more risky to less risky activities). Another potential effect is for exchange rate uncertainty to alter the incentives that consumers and producers have to react to exchange rate changes. The basic idea here is that so long as there are nonrecoverable costs associated with switching suppliers or with entering foreign markets, the response to perceived temporary exchange rate changes will be smaller than the response to perceived permanent changes. Put in other words, exchange rate uncertainty may create an incentive "to wait" that increases with the degree of uncertainty. Employing a similar line of reasoning, the response to small exchange rate changes should then be lower than the response to large ones, since market participants would need to overcome the threshold created by sunk costs.

These potential effects of exchange rate uncertainty could show up in several places. One is in the size of estimated price elasticities of demand for traded goods. *Ceteris paribus*, one would expect these demand price elasticities to be lower during periods of high, short-run exchange rate uncertainty than during periods of lower uncertainty. Unfortunately, comparisons of price elasticities relevant to this question are few and far between.

At this point, probably the most reliable piece of evidence comes from Hooper and Marquez (1993), who survey estimates of price elasticities of demand for imports and exports of the industrial countries. In short, they do find a tendency for import and export price elasticities of demand to be lower, other things equal, in the period of floating exchange rates than in the period of fixed rates.[12] What is not yet clear is whether these lower price elasticities reflect exchange rate uncertainties or other factors. For example, if the weight of high-technology goods in industrial-country exports and imports was increasing over this period, and if these goods carried a lower price elasticity of demand than other categories of trade, a lower aggregate price elasticity might merely represent "compositional" effects. Unfortunately, even less is known about the trade volume responses to large versus small exchange rate changes. Goldstein and Khan (1976) tested whether the price elasticity of demand for aggregate imports of 12 industrial countries varied with the size of the relative price change and found no evidence of such a large/small distinction. That study, however, relied on data drawn almost entirely from the fixed rate period.

A second, more active application is in the area of export pricing. It has often been observed that some exporters seem to be willing to adjust their profit margins rather than fully "pass through" exchange rate changes into their export prices, with the result that local-currency import prices change by less than would otherwise be expected. For example,

---

12. Hooper and Marquez (1993) reach this conclusion after assembling the estimates of price elasticities and then regressing those estimates on a set of characteristics of the underlying studies, including whether the period of estimation was one of floating or fixed exchange rates.

US dollar import prices rose only moderately during 1985–87 in the face of a sharp depreciation of the dollar (Mann 1986).

It has also often been argued that incomplete pass-through of exchange rate changes into local-currency import prices is more likely to occur in exports to some destinations (the United States) than to others (Marston 1990). This is a special case of incomplete pass-through which occurs when export markets can be segmented from one another (that is, when exporters practice price discrimination). This phenomenon of destination-specific adjustment of price markups (over exporters' marginal costs) in response to exchange rate changes has come to be known as "pricing to market" (Krugman 1987a).

There are many potential explanations for incomplete pass-through and for pricing to market—including a nonconstant price elasticity of demand, nonconstant marginal costs of exporters (decreasing returns to scale), and sensitivity of raw material prices to exchange rate changes (Hooper and Marquez 1995). But the more intriguing ones for our purposes are those that are specifically tied to exchange rate uncertainty. Usually, these stories exploit the notion that exporting firms make investments in foreign markets (either in the form of building a sales infrastructure or in purchasing customer allegiance) and that the irreversible nature of these investments, *cum* concerns for protecting market shares, makes it optimal for exporters to "pass through" only a part of exchange rate changes when exchange rates are highly volatile. In any event, researchers have not been able to identify a robust empirical connection between short-run exchange rate variability and pricing-to-market export behavior.

Using data on 65 export industries for five industrial countries over 1981–86, Froot and Klemperer (1989) were unable to find a robust link between the extent of pricing-to-market behavior and the "temporariness" of exchange rate changes. Likewise, Sapir and Sekkat (1990, 10), drawing on a sample of seven industries across five importing and eight exporting countries over 1966–87, concluded that "[short-run exchange rate] volatility had generally no impact on exchange rate pass-through."

More recently, in a quite comprehensive study of export-pricing behavior in four industrial countries, Knetter (1993) found that the critical factor in explaining pricing-to-market behavior was observable "industry" factors rather than either country factors (e.g., the particular destination market for exports, the exporting country) or regime factors. Knetter (1993, 484) concludes that "the lack of an important U.S. destination effect casts doubt on the empirical importance of explanations of PTM (pricing to market) that rely on features of the exchange rate process (e.g., distinctions between temporary and permanent or large versus small changes)."

Exchange Rate Uncertainty and Investment

As on the trade side, it has often been argued that exchange rate volatility has impeded investment in industrial countries. The Bretton Woods Commission (1994a, 6), for example, in parceling out responsibility for disappointing long-term economic performance during the floating rate period, mentions, among other factors, that "since the end of the par value system, efficient growth and investment were hampered by highly variable exchange rates. . . ."

In assessing the past influence of exchange rate volatility on investment and growth in industrial countries, it is useful to keep three considerations in mind.

First of all, the change in investment ratios for industrial countries as between the fixed and floating rate periods has apparently been rather modest. For G-7 countries, the decline, according to IMF figures, is about 1 percent.[13] Similarly, if we examine industrial countries as a group, the change in investment ratios between 1950–73 (or 1960–72) and 1974–94 is small—and may even be positive. Eichengreen and Kenen (1994) cite figures on total gross domestic investment that would put the decline at roughly 1½ percent. On the other side, Shigehara (1993), drawing on an OECD series on business-sector capital, labor, output, and total factor productivity in 22 industrial countries, reports that both nominal and real investment (relative to GDP) were actually slightly higher (by 1 to 2 percent) in 1973–90 than in 1960–73.[14]

Second, the investment ratio for the floating rate period is very much in line with that recorded by industrial countries during other parts of this century (table 7). In this sense, it is the Bretton Woods period that is an "outlier" in terms of its investment performance—not the floating rate period.

Third and most important, to imply that exchange rate volatility could have a *large* negative impact on industrial-country growth performance via its adverse effect on investment is to give insufficient attention to the fundamentals of growth accounting. A few calculations will illustrate the point.

Suppose, implausibly, that *all* of the decline in G-7 investment rates between the fixed and floating rate periods was due to the higher short-run exchange rate volatility of the latter regime. How much could this reduce industrial-country growth rates?

---

13. The G-7 investment ratio for 1960–73 was 21.6 percent, versus 20.5 percent for 1974–94.

14. Business-sector output is measured as real GDP (at market prices) less output originating in general government as measured by the national accounts. Interestingly enough, Englander and Gurney (1994), using the same OECD series, report that despite this slight increase in investment rates, the annual average percentage change in the capital stock (gross real investment less estimated scrapping) during the floating rate period was actually about 2½ percent less than in the last decade of Bretton Woods. Perhaps the higher scrapping rates in the floating rate period have something to do with the effect of large changes in energy prices. Since I am not aware of arguments relating scrapping rates to short-run exchange rate variability, the discussion above sticks to investment rates.

Table 7 Total gross domestic investment as a percentage of GNP in selected industrial countries, 1900–93 (period averages)

Country	1900-13	1914-49	1950-60	1961-71	1972-82	1983-93
Western Europe	..	..	21.0	23.2	21.7	19.9
Belgium	..	..	16.5	21.0	20.9	17.1
France	..	..	19.1	24.6	22.3	20.1
West Germany	..	14.3	24.0	26.0	21.4	20.2
Italy	15.4	13.5	20.8	20.4	19.9	20.3
Netherlands	..	..	24.2	25.6	20.7	20.1
Norway	12.7	15.4	26.4	26.9	30.3	24.3
Sweden	12.3	15.5	21.3	23.0	20.4	19.2
United Kingdom	7.7	7.6	15.4	18.3	18.0	17.5
Canada	25.5	16.0	24.8	22.2	22.7	20.4
Japan	..	..	24.0	35.1	32.1	29.6
United States	20.6	14.7	19.1	16.8	18.2	17.2

.. = not available

Source: Eichengreen and Kenen (1994).

A simple place to start is with a Cobb-Douglas aggregate production function. This implies that the percentage change in the growth rate will be equal to the product of capital's share in output and the percentage change in the capital stock. The share of capital in output in most industrial countries is on the order of one-third (table 8). Because the capital-to-output ratio is greater than one in industrial countries, a 1 percent change in the investment share will lead to less than a 1 percent change in the capital stock. Following Auerbach (1993), suppose we assume that the capital-to-output ratio is 2.5. Then, a 1 percent decline in an economy's investment share (I/Y) would be associated with a decline of 0.40 percent in the capital stock. Multiplying this by capital's share in output yields the conclusion that a 1 percent drop in the industrial-country investment share leads to approximately a 0.13 percent decline in the industrial-country growth rate. This can be compared to the decline in average industrial-country growth rates between the fixed and floating rate periods of approximately 2.5 percent.

An alternative formulation that brings in the rate of return to new investment yields similar conclusions. Following De Long and Summers (1993), one can express the instantaneous change in an economy's growth rate as the product of two things: the change in the share of output that is invested and the social rate of return on the investment. Suppose (optimistically) that this rate of return is roughly 15 percent. Then a 1 percent decrease in the investment share would translate into a decline in the growth rate of 0.15 percent (15 basis points). But even this exagger-

Table 8 Share of capital in output

Country	Business sector, 1961–90[a]	Entire economy, 1973–82[b]
United States	0.32	0.27
Japan	0.31	0.29
Germany	0.33	0.30
France	0.35	0.31
Italy	0.36	..
United Kingdom	0.31	0.26
Canada	0.37	..
Austria	0.34	..
Belgium	0.30	..
Denmark	0.31	..
Finland	0.36	..
Greece	0.37	..
Iceland	0.34	..
Ireland	0.34	..
Netherlands	0.34	0.30
Norway	0.34	..
Portugal	0.42	..
Spain	0.35	..
Sweden	0.30	..
Switzerland	0.29	..
Australia	0.36	..
New Zealand	0.35	..

.. = not available.

Sources: a. Englander and Gurney (1994).
b. Plosser (1993).

ates the final effect on growth because diminishing returns set in as capital is accumulated and because capital depreciation reduces the growth rate of the capital stock. According to De Long and Summers (1993), based on the US experience, the final effect on growth will be approximately one-half of the initial effect—that is, approximately 8 basis points for a 1 percent fall in the investment share. On this calculation, even if all the decline in the investment share between the fixed and floating rate periods were attributable to the adverse effects of higher short-run exchange rate variability, that decline would have accounted for only about *one-thirtieth* of the average growth rate decline between the two periods. De Long and Summers (1993) estimate that (with a 15 percent social rate of return on new investment) it would take an increase of 24 percentage points in the investment share to restore industrial-country growth rates to the average of the 1960s.

All this is but another illustration of how limited are the growth effects of changes in the *quantity* of investment alone. To get much bigger growth effects from increasing capital, one either has to assume that investment is focused on projects with supranormal rates of return, or that investment has important spillover effects on total factor productivity, or that capital is much more broadly defined to include human as well as physical capital (Plosser 1993; Mankiw 1993).

As with the effects of exchange rate uncertainty on trade, economic theory is ambiguous with respect to whether increased exchange rate uncertainty raises or lowers investment. As suggested in the earlier discussion of pricing to market, if investment is irreversible, if there is uncertainty over future returns, and if there is some leeway about the timing of investment, then increased uncertainty increases the option value of waiting (Dixit and Pindyck 1994). This should raise the required rate of return and reduce investment in the short term. On the other hand, Abel (1983) illustrates how profit convexity in prices can lead higher uncertainty to increase investment. In the end, as emphasized by Pindyck and Solimano (1993), economic theory can say little about the effect of an increase in volatility on the long-term, steady-state level of investment (or on the investment-to-output ratio).[15]

This lack of guidance from theory again puts a premium on empirical evidence. But in contrast to the empirical literature on trade, there is very little empirical work for industrial countries on the effect of short-term exchange rate variability on investment. What is available has appeared mainly during the past two or three years.

Goldberg (1993) has examined the effect of short-run exchange rate variability on investment in US manufacturing and nonmanufacturing industries (at both the aggregate and disaggregate level) over 1970–89. In addition to (real) exchange rate volatility, the explanatory variables are the level of real GDP, the cost of capital, and the level of the (real) exchange rate. In brief, she finds that the effects of volatility are "mixed," varying across time and across industries, and even in sign. Negative effects of volatility on investment showed up more frequently in the 1980s than in the 1970s, but even then, these effects are characterized by the author as "quantitatively small."

At this point, the most comprehensive examination of the effects of economic instability on aggregate investment is that of Pindyck and Solimano (1993). They look, inter alia, at the behavior of aggregate investment ratios in a sample of 30 countries (16 developing and 14 OECD countries) over 1960–90. In a first set of regressions, they relate the behavior of private investment ratios over decade-long periods to, inter alia, a measure of the volatility of the marginal profitability of capital. Their results show

---

15. Pindyck and Solimano (1993) note that, whereas (with irreversibility of investment and leeway on the timing of that investment) increased volatility increases the required rate of return needed to trigger investment, it is not known what it will do to the average realized rate of return.

a negative relationship between the two for the full sample of countries, but the estimated coefficient on the volatility variable is significant only for the developing countries. Indeed, the variable carries the wrong sign in the regressions for the OECD countries.

In a second set of regressions, they attempt to isolate the sources of instability in marginal profitability of capital by relating their index to a collection of economic and political variables. Included in the economic group are the mean rate of inflation, the variability of inflation, and the variability of the real exchange rate. In short, they discover that the mean inflation rate is the only variable that is consistently significant as an explanator of the volatility of the marginal profitability of capital.

Finally, in a third set of regressions, they relate the annual (time-series) behavior of the aggregate investment to GDP ratio to the same three measures of economic instability, while controlling for the effects of other factors affecting investment. Regressions are estimated for a sample of low-inflation industrial countries (France, Germany, Japan, the Netherlands, the United Kingdom, and the United States) as well as for a sample of higher-inflation developing countries (Argentina, Bolivia, Brazil, Chile, Israel, and Mexico). For the industrial-country sample, the mean inflation rate again emerges as a negative influence on investment; it is the only one of the instability variables that is consistently significant in all the regressions. The volatility of the real exchange rate is statistically significant with a negative sign when either the mean inflation rate or the variability of inflation is dropped from the regression. In the developing-country sample, the results indicate that inflation, and to a lesser extent the variability of real exchange rates, matter for investment. A recent further set of empirical studies on investment behavior in developing countries (Serven and Solimano 1993) tells a similar story.

I interpret the Pindyck-Solimano results as suggesting that economic instability in general, and short-run variability of real exchange rates in particular, are likely to be much more serious impediments to investment in developing countries than in industrial ones. As argued by Fischer (1993), high and unstable rates of inflation may well be regarded as demonstrating an inability of the government to control the economy, and this may explain its dominance in the regression results for investment, particularly for developing countries.

In addition to effects on domestic investment, it has sometimes been argued that exchange rate variability might prompt greater foreign direct investment, either because international investment diversification allows multinational enterprises to achieve ex post production flexibility and higher profits in response to shocks (Aizenmann 1992), or because higher exchange rate variability will prompt risk-averse investors to locate a higher share of production abroad. Again, empirical evidence that would allow one to evaluate the significance of these theoretical arguments is sparse.

Cushman (1985, 1988), analyzing US bilateral FDI outflows over 1963–78 and inflows over 1963–86, found that exchange rate variability was positively correlated with these flows. In contrast, Bailey and Tavlas (1991), examining FDI flows during 1976–86, could find no association between these flows and short-run exchange rate variability. Morsink and Molle (1991) discovered that direct investment flows among European countries in the 1970s and 1980s were negatively related to short-run exchange rate variability when zero investment flows were included in the sample, but not when the sample was restricted to nonzero flows. In the end, they concluded that exchange rate variability impeded direct investment. Finally, Goldberg and Kolstad (1994) undertook an empirical study of bilateral FDI flows between the United States and the United Kingdom, Canada, and Japan over 1978–91. Their main conclusion is that, *ceteris paribus*, higher exchange rate volatility increases the share of productive capacity located abroad.

Given the paucity of empirical studies and the conflicting findings among them, I would say that it remains an open question if and how short-run exchange rate volatility affects foreign direct investment. In this connection, it is relevant to note that Graham and Krugman's (1995) recent analysis of foreign direct investment flows by and to industrial countries does not include exchange rate volatility as one of the main determinants of these flows.

In any case, the welfare consequences of exchange rate volatility on foreign direct investment are not easily captured by volume effects. Cooper (1988), for example, has argued that any globalization of business attributable to higher exchange rate variability is likely to be uneconomic, since it leads to excessive fragmentation of business and a loss of economies of scale. Yet no estimates of the size of these alleged diseconomies associated with exchange rate volatility exist in the literature. Caution is therefore appropriate in drawing conclusions here as well.

Exchange Rate Uncertainty and Economic Growth

The preceding section has argued that it is implausible that the marked decline in industrial-country growth rates as between the fixed and floating exchange rate periods is attributable to a decline in investment ratios induced in turn by higher short-run exchange rate variability. But perhaps there are other channels by which short-run exchange rate variability could impede growth. This section explores that possibility.

Fortunately, the past five years have witnessed a good deal of empirical work into the causes of the slowdown in growth and productivity rates in industrial countries. While much of it remains a mystery, at least four conclusions of that work are relevant for our inquiry.

First, it is likely that some of the growth slowdown in the past two decades stems from faulty measurement, which has biased downward recorded growth rates (Mathews 1982; Bruno and Sachs 1985; Darby 1993). As the share of services and high-tech goods in industrial-country GDP has increased, it has become more difficult to estimate accurately the real value of output (Kahn 1993). Specifically, it is thought that official statistics underestimate improvements in the quality of many high-tech goods, while overstating price increases. In addition, the practice of measuring output in the service sector by hours of input without taking proper account of possible increases in productivity is likewise regarded as leading to a downward bias.

These sources of downward bias are suspected of having become more serious over the past dozen years or so because of higher growth rates in these sectors. Darby (1993) shows that for the United States, the gap between employment growth in the service sector and that in the goods sector is much larger in 1979–89 than in 1965–79. He estimates that this sectoral shift alone could account for an increase in the downward bias in real GDP growth of 0.6 percentage points. Indeed, Darby (1993) has gone so far as to conclude that measurement problems explain most of the growth slowdown in the United States over the past 15 years. Bruno and Sachs (1985) argue that the double-deflation method of computing value added leads to a systematic undermeasurement of output in periods (like the 1970s) when raw material prices rise in relative terms. Other researchers (e.g., Adams et al. 1987; Grubb 1986) concede that these measurement problems overstate the growth slowdown but doubt that they are capable of explaining most of it.

Second, the lower rates of economic growth and of growth per capita (productivity) during the floating rate period are actually much closer to long-term historical averages than are the very high rates of the fixed exchange rate period. In this sense, it is the rapid growth of the fixed rate period that stands out as the aberration that needs to be explained—not the slow growth of the floating rate period.

Table 9 supports that argument. As emphasized by Meltzer (1993) and Adams et al. (1987), long-term growth rates of labor productivity over 80- to 120-year periods for six of the largest industrial countries are close enough to those of the floating rate period to cause one to question whether the two are economically and statistically different.[16]

As for the higher productivity growth rates of the fixed rate period, most observers attribute this to, inter alia, the unusually large opportunities for

16. Ben-David and Papell (1995) test for statistically significant breaks in growth for 74 countries over 1950–90. Among the countries that were not found to have exhibited a significant trend break (negative or positive) were the United States, Canada, and the United Kingdom. More generally, they find that only 55 percent of their 74 countries exhibited a statistically significant trend break sometime during this 40-year period.

Table 9   Rates of growth of productivity: selected industrial countries (percent per annum)

Country	Period	Growth rate per capita product[a]	Growth rate of productivity 1979–90[b]
United States	1839 to 1960–62	1.7	1.4
Japan	1879–81 to 1959–61	2.6	3.0
Germany	1871–75 to 1960–62	1.8	1.6
France	1841–50 to 1960–62	1.8	1.1
United Kingdom	1855–59 to 1957–59	1.4	1.7
Canada	1870–74 to 1960–62	1.8	1.2

Sources: a. Meltzer (1993).
b. De Long and Summers (1993).

catch-up of technology on the part of non-US industrial countries. For example, De Long and Summers (1993) calculate that, corrected for this catch-up or convergence effect, average annual productivity growth in the OECD over 1950–70 would have been about 1.7 percent—versus the 3.3 percent that actually occurred.

A third robust conclusion is that the slowdown in industrial-country growth rates over the floating rate period primarily reflects a decline in total factor productivity, and to a lesser extent accelerated capital obsolescence, rather than a change in labor's input. According to Englander and Gurney's (1994) figures, of the 270 basis-point slowdown in OECD growth rates (of business output) between the fixed and floating rate periods, on the order of 200 basis points seems to represent a slowdown in total factor productivity.[17] As first highlighted by Solow (1957), this dominance of the "residual" in explaining economic growth applies to most historical periods. This means that if short-run exchange rate variability is to explain a significant share of the growth slowdown in industrial countries during the floating rate period, it would need to do so by adversely affecting productivity growth.

This brings us to the fourth conclusion: the growth and productivity slowdown in industrial countries during the floating rate period still calls for a convincing explanation, but *none* of the stories advanced so far ascribes an important role to short-run exchange rate volatility in the final outcome.

Efforts to explain the productivity slowdown have taken several tacks. Early on, the focus was on temporary factors. As outlined in Adams et al. (1987) and Shigehara (1993), this put the emphasis on the sharp increases in oil and raw material prices in the 1970s, sharp upward movements in inflation rates, larger cyclical output gaps, some slowdown in spending

---

17. Adams et al. (1987) reach a similar qualitative conclusion.

on research and development, and more inexperienced workers entering the labor force. But these factors lost their appeal when most of them reversed course during the 1980s while economic growth and productivity either remained sluggish or deteriorated (Khan 1993). Some other traditional factors, such as changes in the capital stock or changes in average years of schooling of the work force, did not solve the puzzle either because they did not change by enough to explain the bulk of the outcome (the capital stock) or because they went in the wrong direction (years of schooling). Some later explanations that focus on structural changes— ranging from the increases in the size and role of governments, to the growing share of services in output, to rigidities in labor markets *cum* external shocks, to differences in the productivity of private and public investments, to the adverse effect of financial instability on resource allocation and on the productivity of investment—either lack as yet broad-based empirical support or are hard to quantify.

Despite the unsettled nature of the debate on the productivity slowdown in industrial countries, it is noteworthy that short-run exchange rate variability has not been proposed as a key element of the story. Indeed, in a recent symposium on this subject sponsored by the Federal Reserve Bank of Kansas City (1993), I could find only one author or discussant out of 20 (Shigehara 1993) who made any explicit mention of the exchange rate regime in discussing the slowdown. The closest others got to it were references to good macroeconomic performance, or to price stability, or to central bank independence, or to stability in financial markets more generally, as contributing to better growth and productivity performance.[18]

Some recent empirical research (Coe and Helpman 1993; Coe et al. 1994) has highlighted the role of international trade as an important carrier of productivity gains, but this takes place in the form of R&D spillovers— with no apparent link to the variability of exchange rates. Adopting a wider perspective, the secrets to faster growth are generally regarded as lying along more traditional lines. As summarized by Mankiw (1993), the four most robust instructions are: start from behind, save and invest, educate the young, and keep population growth low. Similarly, Fischer's (1993) policy prescriptions for growth are to invest in physical capital, infrastructure, and human capital; keep budget deficits small; maintain low and stable inflation rates; avoid an overvalued exchange rate; safeguard openness to international trade; deregulate; privatize; and keep the tax system simple.

---

18. Fixed exchange rates or low short-run exchange rate variability are hardly synonymous with low inflation. Note, for example, that the United States, Japan, and Germany have been among the best performers in keeping inflation low during the floating rate period, and this following a regime of managed floating (see Goldstein and Isard 1992). Flood and Rose (1993) do not find any significant relationship between the short-run volatility of industrial-country exchange rates and either the level or volatility of inflation rates.

Conclusions

In my view, the aforementioned set of evidence, taken as a whole, makes it very unlikely that the high short-run variability of exchange rates has seriously hampered economic performance in the major industrial countries over the past two decades. Robust links are simply not there—be it for international trade, or for investment, or for economic growth. Particularly strong criticism ought to be heaped on the claim that higher short-run exchange rate variability has played a significant role in the halving of industrial-country growth rates (that emerges from a comparison of the last decade of Bretton Woods with the floating rate era).

In the relatively few cases when a statistically significant effect of exchange rate variability on economic performance is found, the size of the effect is typically small, and more often than not, declining over time. The effects on economic performance may well be more important in developing countries (where it may be more closely associated with economic instability more generally), but even there, existing empirical research is as yet too limited to draw strong policy implications.

All of this supports the argument in the text that the main shortcoming of the existing exchange rate system—at least with respect to the key-currency countries that are at the center of the system—falls in the area of misalignments of real exchange rates, not with the short-run variability of those rates. As such, efforts at improving the system should be concentrated on reducing the frequency and severity of misalignments.

References

Abel, Andrew. 1983. "Optimal Investment Under Uncertainty." *American Economic Review* 73: 228–33.

Adams, Charles, Paul Fenton, and Fleming Larsen. 1987. "Potential Output in Major Industrial Countries." International Monetary Fund. *Staff Studies for the World Economic Outlook*. Washington: International Monetary Fund.

Aizenmann, Joshua. 1992. "Exchange Rate Flexibility, Volatility, and Patterns of Domestic and Foreign Direct Investment." *IMF Staff Papers* 39.

Alesina, Alberto, and Lawrence Summers. 1991. "Central Bank Independence and Macroeconomic Performance: Some Comparative Evidence." Cambridge: Harvard University. Unpublished paper.

Auerbach, Alan. 1993. "Investment Policies to Promote Growth." In Federal Reserve Bank of Kansas City, *Policies for Long-Run Economic Growth*. Kansas City: Federal Reserve Bank of Kansas City.

Bailey, M., and George Tavlas. 1991. "Exchange Rate Variability and Direct Investment." *The Annals AAPSS* 516 (July): 106–16.

Balassa, Bela, and John Williamson. 1987. *Adjusting to Success: Balance of Payments Policy in the East Asian NICs*. Washington: Institute for International Economics.

Bayoumi, Tamim, Peter Clark, Steve Symansky, and Mark Taylor. 1994. "The Robustness of Equilibrium Exchange Rate Calculations to Alternative Assumptions and Methodologies." In John Williamson, *Estimating Equilibrium Exchange Rates*. Washington: Institute for International Economics.

Ben-David, Dan, and David Papell. 1995. *Slowdowns and Meltdowns: Postwar Growth Evidence from 74 Countries*. CEPR Discussion Paper No. 1111. London: Centre for Economic Policy Research.

Bergsten, C. Fred. 1994a. "Managing the World Economy of the Future." In Peter Kenen, *Managing the World Economy: Fifty Years After Bretton Woods*. Washington: Institute for International Economics.

Bergsten, C. Fred. 1994b. "An International Monetary Fund for the 21st Century." Paper presented at IMF/World Bank Conference, Fifty Years After Bretton Woods, Madrid, September.

Bergsten, C. Fred, and C. Randall Henning. 1995. *Mismanaging the World Economy: The Demise of the G-7.* Washington: Institute for International Economics. Forthcoming.

Bergsten, Fred, and John Williamson. 1994. "Is the Time Ripe for Target Zones or the Blueprint?" In Bretton Woods Commission, *Bretton Woods: Looking to the Future.* Conference Proceedings. Washington: Bretton Woods Commission.

Bretton Woods Commission. 1994a. *Bretton Woods: Looking to the Future.* Commission Report, Staff Review, Background Papers. Washington: Bretton Woods Commission.

Bretton Woods Commission. 1994b. *Bretton Woods: Looking to the Future.* Conference Proceedings. Washington: Bretton Woods Commission.

Bruno, Michael, and Jeffrey Sachs. 1985. *The Economics of Worldwide Stagflation.* Cambridge: Harvard University Press.

Bryant, Ralph, Peter Hooper, and Catherine Mann. 1993. "Introduction and Overview." In Ralph Bryant, Peter Hooper, and Catherine Mann, *Evaluating Policy Regimes: New Research in Empirical Macroeconomics.* Washington: Brookings Institution.

Camdessus, Michel. 1994a. "The IMF at Fifty—An Evolving Role but a Constant Mission." Speech at the Institute for International Economics, Washington, DC, June.

Camdessus, Michel. 1994b. "The Future of the IMF." In Bretton Woods Commission, *Bretton Woods: Looking to the Future.* Conference Proceedings. Washington: Bretton Woods Commission.

Camdessus, Michel. 1994c. "Closing Address." IMF/World Bank Conference, "Fifty Years After Bretton Woods," Madrid, September.

Catte, Pietro, Giampaolo Galli, and Salvatore Rebecchini. 1994. "Concerted Interventions and the Dollar: An Analysis of Daily Data." In Peter Kenen, Francesco Papadia, and Fabrizio Saccomanni, *The International Monetary System.* Cambridge: Cambridge University Press.

Caves, Richard. 1982. *Multinational Enterprise and Economic Analysis.* Cambridge: Cambridge University Press.

Clark, Peter, and others. 1994. *Exchange Rates and Economic Fundamentals: A Framework for Analysis.* IMF Occasional Paper No. 115. Washington: International Monetary Fund.

Coe, David, and Elhanan Helpman. 1993. "International R&D Spillovers." IMF Working Paper. Washington: International Monetary Fund (November).

Coe, David, Elhanan Helpman, and Alexander Hoffmaister. 1994. "North-South R&D Spillovers." IMF Working Paper. Washington: International Monetary Fund (December).

Commission of the European Communities. 1990. *One Market, One Money.* Brussels: Commission of the European Communities.

Cooper, Richard. 1971. "Currency Devaluation in Developing Countries." *Essays in International Finance,* No. 86. Princeton, NJ: International Finance Section, Princeton University.

Cooper, Richard. 1988. "Toward an International Commodity Standard?" *Cato Journal* 8 (Fall): 315–38.

Cooper, Richard. 1994. "Comment on Managing the Monetary System." In Peter Kenen, *Managing the World Economy: Fifty Years After Bretton Woods.* Washington: Institute for International Economics.

Crockett, Andrew. 1994. "Monetary Policy Implications of Increased Capital Flows." In Federal Reserve Bank of Kansas City, *Changing Capital Markets: Implications for Monetary Policy.* Kansas City: Federal Reserve Bank of Kansas City.

Cushman, David. 1985. "Real Exchange Rate Risk, Expectations, and the Level of Direct Investment." *Review of Economics and Statistics* 67 (May).

Cushman, David. 1988. "Exchange Rate Uncertainty and Foreign Direct Investment in the United States." *Weltwirtschaftliches Archiv* 124: 322–34.

Darby, Michael. 1993. "Causes of Declining Growth." In Federal Reserve Bank of Kansas City, *Policies for Long-Run Economic Growth.* Kansas City: Federal Reserve Bank of Kansas City.

De Grauwe, Paul. 1988. "Exchange Rate Variability and the Slowdown in the Growth of International Trade." *IMF Staff Papers* 35: 63–84.

De Long, Bradford, and Lawrence Summers. 1993. "Macroeconomic Policy and Long-Run Growth." In Federal Reserve Bank of Kansas City, *Policies for Long-Run Economic Growth*. Kansas City: Federal Reserve Bank of Kansas City.

Dini, Lamberto. 1994. "Comment." In Peter Kenen, Francesco Papadia, and Fabrizio Saccomanni, *The International Monetary System*. Cambridge: Cambridge University Press.

Dini, Lamberto. 1995. "Should the IMF Borrow to Meet the Next Crisis?" *International Herald Tribune* (9 February).

Dixit, Avinash, and Robert Pindyck. 1994. *Investment Under Uncertainty*. Princeton, NJ: Princeton University Press.

Dobson, Wendy. 1991. *Economic Policy Coordination: Requiem or Prologue?* POLICY ANALYSES IN INTERNATIONAL ECONOMICS 30. Washington: Institute for International Economics.

Dobson, Wendy. 1994a. "Economic Policy Coordination Institutionalized?" In Bretton Woods Commission, *Bretton Woods: Looking to the Future*. Conference Proceedings. Washington: Bretton Woods Commission.

Dobson, Wendy. 1994b. "Surveillance and the International Monetary System: Ideals and Realities." Paper presented at IMF/World Bank Conference, Fifty Years After Bretton Woods, Madrid, September.

Dominguez, Kathryn, and Jeffrey Frankel. 1993. *Does Foreign Exchange Intervention Work?* Washington: Institute for International Economics.

Dunn, Robert. 1973. *Exchange Rate Rigidity, Investment Distortions, and the Failure of Bretton Woods*. Essays in International Finance No. 97. Princeton, NJ: International Finance Section, Princeton University.

Edison, Hali. 1993. *The Effectiveness of Central-Bank Intervention: A Study of the Literature After 1982*. Special Papers in International Economics, No. 18. Princeton, NJ: International Finance Section, Princeton University.

Edison, Hali, and Michael Melvin. 1990. "The Determinants and Implications of the Choice of an Exchange Rate System." In William Haraf and Thomas Willett, *Monetary Policy for a Volatile Global Economy*. Washington: AEI Press.

Edwards, Sebastian. 1989. *Exchange Rate Misalignment in Developing Countries*. Baltimore: Johns Hopkins University Press.

Edwards, Sebastian. 1994. "Real and Monetary Determinants of Real Exchange Rate Behavior: Theory and Evidence from Developing Countries." In John Williamson, *Estimating Equilibrium Exchange Rates*. Washington: Institute for International Economics.

Eichengreen, Barry. 1994. *International Monetary Arrangements for the 21st Century*. Washington: Brookings Institution.

Eichengreen, Barry, and Douglas Irwin. 1995. "Trade Blocs, Currency Blocs and the Reorientation of World Trade in the 1930s." *Journal of International Economics* 38 (February): 1–24.

Eichengreen, Barry, and Peter Kenen. 1994. "Managing the World Economy under the Bretton Woods System: An Overview." In Peter Kenen, *Managing the World Economy: Fifty Years After Bretton Woods*. Washington: Institute for International Economics.

Englander, Steven, and Andrew Gurney. 1994. "OECD Productivity Growth: Medium-Term Trends." *OECD Economic Studies* 22 (Spring): 111–29.

Fernandez-Arias, Eduardo, and Peter Montiel. 1995. "The Surge in Capital Inflows to Developing Countries: An Overview." Washington: World Bank. Unpublished paper.

Finch, David. 1994. "Governance of the International Monetary Fund by its Members." In Bretton Woods Commission, *Bretton Woods: Looking to the Future*. Conference Proceedings. Washington: Bretton Woods Commission.

Fischer, Stanley. 1993. "Overview." In Federal Reserve Bank of Kansas City, *Policies for Long-Run Economic Growth*. Kansas City: Federal Reserve Bank of Kansas City.

Fischer, Stanley. 1994. "The Mission of the Fund." In Bretton Woods Commission, *Bretton Woods: Looking to the Future*. Conference Proceedings. Washington: Bretton Woods Commission.

Fleming, Marcus. 1970. "Discussion." In Federal Reserve Bank of Boston, *The International Adjustment Mechanism*. Boston: Federal Reserve Bank of Boston.

Flood, Robert, Andrew Rose, and Donald Mathieson. 1991. "An Empirical Examination of Exchange Rate Target Zones." In Allan Meltzer, ed., *Carnegie-Rochester Series on Public Policy* 35: 7–66.

Flood, Robert, and Andrew Rose. 1993. *Fixing Exchange Rates: A Virtual Quest for Fundamentals*. NBER Working Paper No. 4503. Cambridge, MA: National Bureau of Economic Research (October).

Frankel, Jeffrey, and Steven Phillips. 1992. "The European Monetary System: Credible at Last?" *Oxford Economic Papers* 44: 791–816.

Frankel, Jeffrey, and Andrew Rose. 1995. "An Empirical Characterization of Nominal Exchange Rates." In Gene Grossman and Ken Rogoff, *Handbook of International Economics* 3. Amsterdam: North Holland. Forthcoming.

Frankel, Jeffrey, and Shang-Jin Wei. 1995. "European Integration and the Regionalization of World Trade and Currencies." In Barry Eichengreen, Jeffrey Frieden, and Jurgen von Hagen, *Monetary and Fiscal Policy in an Integrated Europe*. New York: Springer-Verlag Press.

Frenkel, Jacob, and Morris Goldstein. 1986. "A Guide to Target Zones." *IMF Staff Papers* 33: 633–73.

Frenkel, Jacob, and Morris Goldstein. 1988. "Exchange Rate Volatility and Misalignment." In Federal Reserve Bank of Kansas City, *Financial Market Volatility*. Kansas City: Federal Reserve Bank of Kansas City.

Frenkel, Jacob, and Morris Goldstein. 1992. "Macroeconomic Implications of Currency Zones." In Federal Reserve Bank of Kansas City, *Policy Implications of Trade and Currency Zones*. Kansas City: Federal Reserve Bank of Kansas City.

Froot, Kenneth, and Paul Klemperer. 1989. "Exchange Rate Pass-Through When Market Share Matters." *American Economic Review* 79 (September): 637–54.

Gagnon, Joseph. 1993. "Exchange Variability and the Level of International Trade." *Journal of International Economics* 34 (May): 269–87.

Garber, Peter, and Michael Spencer. 1995. "Dynamic Hedging and the Interest Rate Defense." In Jeffrey Frankel, Giampaolo Galli, and Alberto Giovannini, *The Microstructure of Foreign Exchange Markets*. Chicago: University of Chicago Press. Forthcoming.

Garber, Peter, and Lars Svensson. 1995. "The Operation and Collapse of Fixed Exchange Rate Regimes." In Gene Grossman and Ken Rogoff, *Handbook of International Economics* 3. Amsterdam: North Holland. Forthcoming.

Garber, Peter, and Mark Taylor. 1995. "Sand in the Wheels of Foreign Exchange Markets: A Skeptical Note." *Economic Journal* 105 (January): 173–80.

Goldberg, Linda. 1993. "Exchange Rates and Investment in United States Industry." *Review of Economics and Statistics* 75 (November): 575–89.

Goldberg, Linda, and Charles Kolstad. 1994. *Foreign Direct Investment, Exchange Rate Variability, and Demand Uncertainty*. NBER Working Paper No. 4815. Cambridge, MA: National Bureau of Economic Research (August).

Goldsborough, David. 1981. "International Trade of Multinational Corporations and Its Responsiveness to Changes in Aggregate Demand and Relative Prices." *IMF Staff Papers* 28: 573–99.

Goldstein, Morris, David Folkerts-Landau, and others. 1993. *International Capital Markets: Part I. Exchange Rate Management and International Capital Flows*. IMF World Economic and Financial Surveys. Washington: International Monetary Fund (April).

Goldstein, Morris, David Folkerts-Landau, and others. 1994. *International Capital Markets: Developments, Prospects and Policy Issues*. IMF World Economic and Financial Surveys. Washington: International Monetary Fund (September).

Goldstein, Morris, and Peter Isard. 1992. "Mechanisms for Promoting Global Monetary Stability." In Morris Goldstein, Peter Isard, Paul Masson, and Mark Taylor, *Policy Issues in the Evolving International Monetary System*. Occasional Paper No. 96. Washington: International Monetary Fund.

Goldstein, Morris, and Mohsin Khan. 1976. "Large and Small Price Changes and the Demand for Imports." *IMF Staff Papers* 23: 200–25.

Goldstein, Morris, and Mohsin Khan. 1985. "Income and Price Effects in Foreign Trade." In Peter Kenen and Ronald Jones, *Handbook of International Economics* 2. Amsterdam: North Holland.

Goldstein, Morris, and Michael Mussa. 1994. "The Integration of World Capital Markets." In Federal Reserve Bank of Kansas City, *Changing Capital Markets: Implications for Monetary Policy*. Kansas City: Federal Reserve Bank of Kansas City.

Graham, Edward M. 1995. *Global Firms and National Governments*. Washington: Institute for International Economics. Forthcoming.

Graham, Edward M., and Paul Krugman. 1995. *Foreign Direct Investment in the United States*. 3rd ed. Washington: Institute for International Economics.

Grant, Richard, Maria Papadakis, and David Richardson. 1993. "Global Trade Flows: Old Structures, New Issues, Empirical Evidence." In C. Fred Bergsten and Marcus Noland, *Pacific Dynamism and the International Economic System*. Washington: Institute for International Economics.

Grilli, Enzo. 1988. "Macroeconomic Determinants of Trade Protection." *The World Economy* 11 (September): 313–26.

Group of Ten Deputies. 1993. *International Capital Movements and Foreign Exchange Markets: Report to the Ministers and Governors by the Group of Ten Deputies*. Rome: Bank of Italy.

Grubb, David. 1986. "Raw Materials, Profits, and the Productivity Slowdown: Some Doubts." *Quarterly Journal of Economics* 101 (February): 175–84.

Gyohten, Toyoo. 1994. "The IMF: A New Role in the Monetary System?" In Bretton Woods Commission, *Bretton Woods: Looking to the Future*. Conference Proceedings. Washington: Bretton Woods Commission.

Hakkio, Craig. 1994. "Should We Throw Sand in the Gears of Financial Markets?" Federal Reserve Bank of Kansas City, *Economic Review* (Second Quarter): 17–30.

Haller, Gert. 1994. "The Future of the IMF." In Bretton Woods Commission, *Bretton Woods: Looking to the Future*. Conference Proceedings. Washington: Bretton Woods Commission.

Hooper, Peter, and Jaime Marquez. 1993. *Exchange Rates, Prices, and External Adjustment in the United States and Japan*. International Finance Discussion Paper No. 456. Washington: Board of Governors of the Federal Reserve System (October).

International Monetary Fund. 1984a. *Exchange Rate Volatility and the Level of International Trade*. IMF Occasional Paper No. 28. Washington: International Monetary Fund.

International Monetary Fund. 1984b. *Issues in the Assessment of Exchange Rates of Industrial Countries*. IMF Occasional Paper No. 29. Washington: International Monetary Fund.

International Monetary Fund. 1994. *World Economic Outlook*. IMF World Economic and Financial Surveys. Washington: International Monetary Fund (October).

Jurgensen, Phillipe. 1983. "Report of the Working Group on Exchange Market Intervention." Washington: US Treasury.

Kahn, George. 1993. "Symposium Summary." In Federal Reserve Bank of Kansas City, *Policies for Long-Run Economic Growth*. Kansas City: Federal Reserve Bank of Kansas City.

Kenen, Peter. 1992. *EMU After Maastricht*. New York: Group of Thirty.

Kenen, Peter, ed. 1994a. *Managing the World Economy: Fifty Years After Bretton Woods*. Washington: Institute for International Economics.

Kenen, Peter. 1994b. "Ways to Reform Exchange Rate Arrangements." In Bretton Woods Commission, *Bretton Woods: Looking to the Future*. Conference Proceedings. Washington: Bretton Woods Commission.

Kenen, Peter. 1994c. "The Agenda for the Bretton Woods Institutions." Paper presented at IMF/World Bank Conference, "Fifty Years After Bretton Woods," Madrid, September.

Klein, Michael, and Nancy Marion. 1994. *Explaining the Duration of Exchange Rate Pegs*. NBER Working Paper No. 4651. Cambridge, MA: National Bureau of Economic Research (February).

Knetter. Michael. 1993. "International Comparisons of Pricing-to-Market Behavior." *American Economic Review* 83 (June): 473–86.

Krugman, Paul. 1985. "Is the Strong Dollar Sustainable?" In Federal Reserve Bank of Kansas City, *The U.S. Dollar—Recent Developments, Outlook, and Options*. Kansas City: Federal Reserve Bank of Kansas City.

Krugman, Paul. 1987a. "Pricing to Market When the Exchange Rate Changes." In Sven Arndt and David Richardson, *Real Financial Linkages Among Open Economies*. Cambridge: MIT Press.

Krugman, Paul. 1987b. *Trigger Strategies and Price Dynamics in Equity and Foreign Exchange Markets?* NBER Working Paper No. 2459. Cambridge: National Bureau of Economic Research.

Krugman, Paul. 1991a. *Has the Adjustment Process Worked?* POLICY ANALYSES IN INTERNATIONAL ECONOMICS 34. Washington: Institute for International Economics.

Krugman, Paul. 1991b. "Target Zones and Exchange Rate Dynamics." *Quarterly Journal of Economics* 106 (August): 669–82.

Krugman, Paul. 1995. "Growing World Trade: Causes and Consequences." Paper presented to 25th Anniversary Meeting of Brookings Panel on Economic Activity, Washington, DC, April.

Larosiere, Jacques. 1994. "The International Monetary System Fifty Years After Bretton Woods: Looking to the Future." Paper presented at IMF/World Bank Conference, "Fifty Years After Bretton Woods," Madrid, September.

Lewis, Karen. 1995. "Puzzles in International Financial Markets." In Gene Grossman and Ken Rogoff, *Handbook of International Economics* 3. Amsterdam: North Holland. Forthcoming.

McKinnon, Ronald, and Kenichi Ohno. 1988. "Purchasing Power Parity As a Monetary Standard." Paper presented at conference on The Future of the International Monetary System, York University, June.

Maddison, Angus. 1991. *Dynamic Forces in Capitalist Development*. Oxford: Oxford University Press.

Makin, John. 1974. *Capital Flows and Exchange Rate Flexibility in the Post Bretton Woods Era*. Essays in International Finance No. 103. Princeton, NJ: International Finance Section, Princeton University.

Mankiw, Gregory. 1993. "Commentary on The Search for Growth." In Federal Reserve Bank of Kansas City, *Policies for Long-Run Economic Growth*. Kansas City: Federal Reserve Bank of Kansas City.

Mann, Catherine. 1986. "Prices, Profit Margins, and Exchange Rates." *Federal Reserve Bulletin* 72 (June): 366–79.

Marston, Richard. 1988. *Misalignment of Exchange Rates: Effects on Trade and Industry*. Chicago: University of Chicago Press.

Marston, Richard. 1990. "Pricing to Market in Japanese Manufacturing." *Journal of International Economics* 29 (December): 217–36.

Mathews, R. C. O. 1982. *Slower Growth in the Western World*. London: Heinemann.

Mathieson, Donald, and Liliana Rojas-Suarez. 1993. "Liberalization of the Capital Account." IMF Occasional Paper No. 103. Washington: International Monetary Fund.

Meese, Richard, and Ken Rogoff. 1983a. "Empirical Exchange Rate Models of the Seventies: Do They Fit Out of Sample?" *Journal of International Economics* 14 (February): 3–24.

Meese, Richard, and Ken Rogoff. 1983b. "The Out-of-Sample Failure of Empirical Exchange Rate Models." In Jacob Frenkel, *Exchange Rates and International Macroeconomics*. Chicago: University of Chicago Press.

Meltzer, Allan. 1993. "Commentary on Macroeconomic Policy and Economic Growth." In Federal Reserve Bank of Kansas City, *Policies for Long-Run Economic Growth*. Kansas City: Federal Reserve Bank of Kansas City.

Morsink, R. L., and W. T. Molle. 1991. "Direct Investments and Monetary Integration." In Commission of the European Communities, *The Economics of EMU*. Brussels: Commission of the European Communities.

Mussa, Michael. 1986. "Nominal Exchange Rate Regimes and the Behavior of Real Exchange Rates." In Karl Brunner and Allan Meltzer, *Real Business Cycles, Real Exchange Rates, and Actual Policies*. Carnegie-Rochester Conference Series on Public Policy, No. 25. Amsterdam: North Holland.

Mussa, Michael. 1990. *Exchange Rates in Theory and Reality*. Essays in International Finance, No. 179. Princeton, NJ: International Finance Section, Princeton University.

Mussa, Michael, and Peter Isard. 1993. "A Note on the Variability of Nominal and Real Exchange Rates." In Group of Ten Deputies, *International Capital Movements and Foreign Exchange Markets: Report to the Ministers and Governors by the Group of Ten Deputies*. Rome: Bank of Italy.

Mussa, Michael, Morris Goldstein, Peter Clark, Donald Mathieson, and Tamim Bayoumi. 1994a. *Improving the International Monetary System: Constraints and Possibilities*. IMF Occasional Paper No. 116. Washington: International Monetary Fund (December).

Mussa, Michael, and others. 1994b. "Observations and Issues Concerning International Policy Coordination." Washington: International Monetary Fund. Unpublished paper.

Nakahira, Kosuke. 1994. "The Future of the IMF." In Bretton Woods Commission, *Bretton Woods: Looking to the Future*. Conference Proceedings. Washington: Bretton Woods Commission.

Nurkse, Ragnar. 1945. "Conditions of International Monetary Equilibrium." *Essays in International Finance*, no. 4. Princeton, NJ: International Finance Section, Princeton University.

Obstfeld, Maurice. 1990. "The Effectiveness of Foreign-Exchange Intervention: Recent Experience, 1985–88." In William Branson, Jacob Frenkel, and Morris Goldstein, *International Policy Coordination and Exchange Rate Fluctuations*. Chicago: University of Chicago Press.

Obstfeld, Maurice. 1995. "International Currency Experience: New Lessons and Lessons Relearned." Paper presented to 25th Anniversary Meeting of Brookings Panel on Economic Activity, Washington, DC, April.

Ohno, Kenichi. 1994. "The Case for a New System." In Bretton Woods Commission, *Bretton Woods: Looking to the Future*. Conference Proceedings. Washington: Bretton Woods Commission.

Pindyck, Robert, and Andres Solimano. 1993. *Economic Instability and Aggregate Investment*. Policy Research Working Paper No. 1148. Washington: World Bank (June).

Plosser, Charles. 1993. "The Search for Growth." In Federal Reserve Bank of Kansas City, *Policies for Long-Run Economic Growth*. Kansas City: Federal Reserve Bank of Kansas City.

Sachs, Jeffrey. 1994. "The IMF and Economies in Crisis." Unpublished paper (August).

Santer, Jacques. 1995. "Interview." *La Tribune* (24 April).

Sapir, Andre, and Khalid Sekkat. 1990. "Exchange Rate Volatility and International Trade." In Paul De Grawwe and Lucas Papedemos, *The European Monetary System in the 1990s*. London: Longman.

Sapir, Andre, Khalid Sekkat, and Axel Weber. 1994. *The Impact of Exchange Rate Fluctuations on European Union Trade*. CEPR Discussion Paper No. 1041. London: Centre for Economic Policy Research (November).

Schulmann, Horst. 1994. "Comment on Managing the World Economy of the Future." In Peter Kenen, *Managing the World Economy: Fifty Years After Bretton Woods*. Washington: Institute for International Economics.

Serven, Luis, and Andres Solimano. 1993. *Striving for Growth After Adjustment*. Washington: World Bank.

Shigehara, Kumihara. 1993. "Causes of Declining Growth in Industrialized Countries." In Federal Reserve Bank of Kansas City, *Policies for Long-Run Economic Growth*. Kansas City: Federal Reserve Bank of Kansas City.

Shultz, George. 1995. *Economics in Action: Ideas, Institutions, Policies*. Essays in Public Policy, No. 58. Palo Alto, CA: Hoover Institution, Stanford University.

Solomon, Robert. 1994. "The Uncertain Future of the Exchange Rate Regime." Paper presented at conference, "Bretton Woods Revisited." Bretton Woods, NH, October.

Solow, Robert. 1957. "Technological Change and the Aggregate Production Function." *Review of Economics and Statistics* 39: 312–20.

Stein, Jerome. 1994. "The Natural Real Exchange Rate of the US Dollar and Determinants of Capital Flows." In John Williamson, *Estimating Equilibrium Exchange Rates*. Washington: Institute for International Economics.

Summers, Lawrence. 1994a. "Future of the IMF." In Bretton Woods Commission, *Bretton Woods: Looking to the Future*. Conference Proceedings. Washington: Bretton Woods Commission.

Summers, Lawrence. 1994b. "Shared Prosperity and the New International Economic Order." In Peter Kenen, *Managing the World Economy: Fifty Years After Bretton Woods*. Washington: Institute for International Economics.

Svensson, Lars. 1992. "An Interpretation of Recent Research on Exchange Rate Target Zones." *Journal of Economic Perspectives* 6, no. 4 (Fall): 119–44.

Tanzi, Vito. 1988. "Fiscal Policy and International Coordination." Paper presented to conference on Fiscal Policy, Economic Adjustment, and Financial Markets, Boconni University, January.

Trichet, Jean-Claude. 1994. "The International Monetary Regime: Enhanced Coordination to Promote Stability." In Bretton Woods Commission, *Bretton Woods: Looking to the Future*. Conference Proceedings. Washington: Bretton Woods Commission.

Truman, Edward. 1994. "Comment on Concerted Interventions and the Dollar." In Peter Kenen, Francesco Papadia, and Fabrizio Saccomanni, *The International Monetary System*. Cambridge: Cambridge University Press.

United Nations Commission on Trade and Development (UNCTAD). 1994. *World Investment Report, 1994*. Geneva: United Nations.

US Treasury Department. 1993. *Sixth Annual Report to the Congress on International Economic and Exchange Rate Policy*. Washington: US Treasury Department (December).

Volcker, Paul. 1994. "Comment." In Peter Kenen, *Managing the World Economy: Fifty Years After Bretton Woods*. Washington: Institute for International Economics.

Volcker, Paul, and Toyoo Gyohten. 1992. *Changing Fortunes*. New York: Times Books.

Williamson, John. 1985. *The Exchange Rate System*, rev. POLICY ANALYSES IN INTERNATIONAL ECONOMICS 5. Washington: Institute for International Economics.

Williamson, John. 1994a. *Estimating Equilibrium Exchange Rates*. Washington: Institute for International Economics.

Williamson, John. 1994b. "Estimates of FEERs." In John Williamson, *Estimating Equilibrium Exchange Rates*. Washington: Institute for International Economics.

Williamson, John, and Stephan Haggard. 1994. "The Political Conditions for Economic Reform." In John Williamson, *The Political Economy of Policy Reform*. Washington: Institute for International Economics.

Williamson, John, and C. Randall Henning. 1994. "Managing the Monetary System." In Peter Kenen, *Managing the World Economy: Fifty Years After Bretton Woods*. Washington: Institute for International Economics.

Williamson, John, and Marcus Miller. 1987. *Targets and Indicators: A Blueprint for the International Coordination of Economic Policy*. POLICY ANALYSES IN INTERNATIONAL ECONOMICS 22. Washington: Institute for International Economics.

Wren-Lewis, Simon, and others. 1991. "Evaluating the United Kingdom's Choice of Entry Rate into the ERM." *Manchester School* 59: 1–22.

Other Publications from the
Institute for International Economics

POLICY ANALYSES IN INTERNATIONAL ECONOMICS Series

1 The Lending Policies of the International Monetary Fund
John Williamson/*August 1982*
ISBN paper 0-88132-000-5   72 pp.

2 "Reciprocity": A New Approach to World Trade Policy?
William R. Cline/*September 1982*
ISBN paper 0-88132-001-3   41 pp.

3 Trade Policy in the 1980s
C. Fred Bergsten and William R. Cline/*November 1982*
(out of print)   ISBN paper 0-88132-002-1   84 pp.
Partially reproduced in the book *Trade Policy in the 1980s.*

4 International Debt and the Stability of the World Economy
William R. Cline/*September 1983*
ISBN paper 0-88132-010-2   134 pp.

5 The Exchange Rate System, Second Edition
John Williamson/*September 1983, rev. June 1985*
(out of print)   ISBN paper 0-88132-034-X   61 pp.

6 Economic Sanctions in Support of Foreign Policy Goals
Gary Clyde Hufbauer and Jeffrey J. Schott/*October 1983*
ISBN paper 0-88132-014-5   109 pp.

7 A New SDR Allocation?
John Williamson/*March 1984*
(out of print)   ISBN paper 0-88132-028-5   61 pp.

8 An International Standard for Monetary Stabilization
Ronald I. McKinnon/*March 1984*
(out of print)   ISBN paper 0-88132-018-8   108 pp.

9 The Yen/Dollar Agreement: Liberalizing Japanese Capital Markets
Jeffrey A. Frankel/*December 1984*
ISBN paper 0-88132-035-8   86 pp.

10 Bank Lending to Developing Countries: The Policy Alternatives
C. Fred Bergsten, William R. Cline, and John Williamson/*April 1985*
ISBN paper 0-88132-032-3   221 pp.

11 Trading for Growth: The Next Round of Trade Negotiations
Gary Clyde Hufbauer and Jeffrey J. Schott/*September 1985*
(out of print)   ISBN paper 0-88132-033-1   109 pp.

12 Financial Intermediation Beyond the Debt Crisis
Donald R. Lessard and John Williamson/*September 1985*
(out of print)   ISBN paper 0-88132-021-8   130 pp.

13 The United States-Japan Economic Problem
C. Fred Bergsten and William R. Cline/*October 1985, 2d ed. January 1987*
(out of print)   ISBN paper 0-88132-060-9   180 pp.

Economic Sanctions Reconsidered (in two volumes)
Economic Sanctions Reconsidered: Supplemental Case Histories
Gary Clyde Hufbauer, Jeffrey J. Schott, and Kimberly Ann Elliott/*1985, 2d ed. December 1990*
ISBN cloth 0-88132-115-X 928 pp.
ISBN paper 0-88132-105-2 928 pp.

Economic Sanctions Reconsidered: History and Current Policy
Gary Clyde Hufbauer, Jeffrey J. Schott, and Kimberly Ann Elliott/*December 1990*
ISBN cloth 0-88132-136-2 288 pp.
ISBN paper 0-88132-140-0 288 pp.

Pacific Basin Developing Countries: Prospects for the Future
Marcus Noland/*January 1991*
(out of print) ISBN cloth 0-88132-141-9 250 pp.
ISBN paper 0-88132-081-1 250 pp.

Currency Convertibility in Eastern Europe
John Williamson, editor/*October 1991*
ISBN cloth 0-88132-144-3 396 pp.
ISBN paper 0-88132-128-1 396 pp.

International Adjustment and Financing: The Lessons of 1985-1991
C. Fred Bergsten, editor/*January 1992*
ISBN paper 0-88132-112-5 336 pp.

North American Free Trade: Issues and Recommendations
Gary Clyde Hufbauer and Jeffrey J. Schott/*April 1992*
ISBN cloth 0-88132-145-1 392 pp.
ISBN paper 0-88132-120-6 392 pp.

Narrowing the U.S. Current Account Deficit
Allen J. Lenz/*June 1992*
(out of print) ISBN cloth 0-88132-148-6 640 pp.
ISBN paper 0-88132-103-6 640 pp.

The Economics of Global Warming
William R. Cline/*June 1992*
ISBN cloth 0-88132-150-8 416 pp.
ISBN paper 0-88132-132-X 416 pp.

U.S. Taxation of International Income: Blueprint for Reform
Gary Clyde Hufbauer, assisted by Joanna M. van Rooij/*October 1992*
ISBN cloth 0-88132-178-8 304 pp.
ISBN paper 0-88132-134-6 304 pp.

Who's Bashing Whom? Trade Conflict in High-Technology Industries
Laura D'Andrea Tyson/*November 1992*
ISBN cloth 0-88132-151-6 352 pp.
ISBN paper 0-88132-106-0 352 pp.

Korea in the World Economy
Il SaKong/*January 1993*
ISBN cloth 0-88132-184-2 328 pp.
ISBN paper 0-88132-106-0 328 pp.

Pacific Dynamism and the International Economic System
C. Fred Bergsten and Marcus Noland, editors/*May 1993*
ISBN paper 0-88132-196-6 424 pp.

SPECIAL REPORTS

WORKS IN PROGRESS

The list below describes research in progress at the Institute. It is intended to inform our customers about our current research agenda. We do not accept back orders for books in this section because of the uncertainty about publication dates.

Mismanaging the World Economy: The Demise of the G-7
C. Fred Bergsten and C. Randall Henning

Trade, Jobs, and Income Distribution
William R. Cline

Environment in the New World Order
Daniel C. Esty

Trade and Labor Standards
Kimberly Ann Elliott and Richard Freeman

Regionalism and Globalism in the World Economic System
Jeffrey A. Frankel

APEC and Japan
Yoichi Funabashi

Overseeing Global Capital Markets
Morris Goldstein and Peter Garber

Global Competition Policy
Edward M. Graham and J. David Richardson

Global Firms and National Governments
Edward M. Graham

Toward an Asia Pacific Economic Community?
Gary Clyde Hufbauer and Jeffrey J. Schott

The Economics of Korean Unification
Marcus Noland

The Case for Trade: A Modern Reconsideration
J. David Richardson

Managing Official Export Credits
John E. Ray

The Future of the World Trading System
John Whalley, in collaboration with Colleen Hamilton

Standards and Conformity Assessment in APEC
John Wilson